REBEL-*in*-CHIEF

REBEL
-in-
CHIEF

Inside the Bold and Controversial

Presidency of George W. Bush

FRED BARNES

CROWN
FORUM
NEW YORK

Copyright © 2006 by Fred Barnes

Published in the United States by Crown Forum, an imprint of the
Crown Publishing Group, a division of Random House, Inc.,
New York.
www.crownpublishing.com

Crown Forum and the Crown Forum colophon are trademarks of
Random House, Inc.

Library of Congress Cataloging-in-Publication Data

Barnes, Fred, 1943–
   Rebel-in-chief : inside the bold and controversial presidency of
George W. Bush / Fred Barnes.—1st ed.
      p.   cm.
   Includes index.
   1. United States—Politics and government—2001–   2. United
States—Foreign relations—2001–   3. Bush, George W. (George
Walker), 1946—Political and social views.   4. Bush, George W.
(George Walker), 1946—Influence.   5. Conservatism—United
States.   I. title.
   E902.B3725 2006
   973.931'092—dc22   2005023362

ISBN-13: 978-0-307-33649-1
ISBN-10: 0-307-33649-2

Printed in the United States of America

Design by Lenny Henderson

10   9   8   7   6   5   4   3   2   1

First Edition

To Barbara

Contents

Contents

Chapter 9
The New Conservatism

Chapter 10
The New Majority

Epilogue
A Rebel's Legacy

REBEL-*in*-CHIEF

Chapter 1

The Insurgent Leader

IT'S FEBRUARY 2, 2005, and President George W. Bush has a lot on his mind. In a matter of hours he'll deliver the State of the Union address in the chamber of the House of Representatives in the Capitol. The speech will set both the tone and the agenda for his second White House term. And, as always, it will be nationally televised and watched worldwide as well. He's practiced the speech twice before on a TelePrompTer and may once more.

His priorities are bold and controversial. Two weeks ago, in his inaugural address, he announced a crusade to uproot tyranny and plant democracy around the world. Many American and foreign political leaders, plus the usual horde of media commentators, found the idea grandiose or simply naïve. So the president needs to flesh out his ambitious plan convincingly. As luck would have it—and Bush's luck is legendary—his task has been made easier by the breathtaking success of the election in Iraq two days earlier. Before the election, the Washington press corps expected little from the Iraqis. A *Washington Post* reporter, Dana Milbank, suggested sarcastically that the Iraqi turnout at the polls might number only in the dozens. He was off by 8.5 million.

Bush has other big issues to talk about besides Iraq. He wants to privatize Social Security partially and make the wobbly system solvent for generations to come; he wants to overhaul the tax code; he wants to tilt the ideological balance of the federal courts to the right; and he wants to inject free-market forces into America's dysfunctional health care system.

For now, though, the president has to attend an off-the-record lunch in the White House study adjacent to the State Dining Room. "Why do I have to go to this meeting?" Bush asks his communications director, Dan Bartlett. "It's traditional," Bartlett explains. Indeed, for years, the president has hosted the TV news anchors for lunch on the day of the State of the Union address. It's an invitation the anchors eagerly accept. Peter Jennings and George Stephanopoulos of ABC, Tom Brokaw and Brian Williams of NBC, Chris Wallace and Brit Hume of Fox, and Wolf Blitzer and Judy Woodruff of CNN will be there. So will Dan Rather of CBS, magnanimously invited in spite of having sought to derail the president's reelection campaign by spotlighting four documents (later proved to be fabrications) that indicated Bush had used political pull to get into the Texas Air National Guard and avoid Vietnam duty, and that he had been honorably discharged without fully completing his service. (At the lunch, Rather will suddenly appear solicitous of Bush. "Thank you, Mr. President," he will say as he leaves. "Thank you, Mr. President." Bush will betray no hint of satisfaction.)

Bush's dread of the lunch is understandable. With few

exceptions—Hume is one—the anchors are faithful purveyors of the conventional wisdom, which is usually gloomy regarding outcomes that might cast Bush in a good light. It is also tinged with liberalism, and wrong. The president agrees with practically none of it.

Sure enough, once the lunch meeting begins, the president takes issue with many of the anchors' claims. Stephanopoulos suggests congressional Republicans rightly fear that Social Security reform will hurt them in the 2006 midterm election. "You don't understand the politics of the issue," Bush responds. Woodruff says that critics worry the president is resolved to take on tyrannies everywhere. "I wasn't aware that was a criticism," Bush answers sarcastically. Jennings says an American general in Iraq told him that the Syrians are helpful there. "I'd like to talk to that general," Bush says in disbelief. In fact, the Syrians are nothing but trouble, he adds, and have been all along. Bush chastises his media guests for negativism. "Nobody around this table thought the elections were going to go that well in Afghanistan, Palestine, Ukraine, and Iraq." And they darn well should understand that he intends to dominate Washington and impose his priorities: "If the president doesn't set the agenda," Bush declares firmly, "it'll be set for you."

Bush's conduct at the lunch—edgy, blunt, self-confident, a bit smart-alecky, disdainful of what the media icons are peddling—is typical. In private or public, he is defiant of the press, scornful of the conventional wisdom, and keen to reverse or at least substantially reform long-standing policies like support for undemocratic but friendly autocracies and the no-tinkering approach to Social Security. Stephanopoulos's notion about potential political harm from seeking to reform Social Security, Bush says, is thirty years behind the times.

Years ago, Donald Rumsfeld answered a reporter's query by saying, "First let me unravel the flaws in your question." Bush has adopted a less bellicose version of the Rumsfeld model. Not surprisingly, he was drawn to Rumsfeld personally. In picking a defense secretary, Bush was initially inclined to go with former senator Dan Coats of Indiana. But he wanted someone who would stand up to Secretary of State Colin Powell and Vice President Dick Cheney in national security deliberations. He turned to a certifiable tough guy— Rumsfeld. Coats became ambassador to Germany.

REBEL

President Bush operates in Washington like the head of a small occupying army of insurgents, an elected band of brothers (and quite a few sisters) on a mission. He's an alien in the realm of the governing class, given a green card by voters. He's a different kind of president in style and substance.

He'd rather invite his first envoy to Iraq, L. Paul Bremer, and his wife, Francie, to a quiet evening at the White House than appear at a Washington gala or social event. The night before the White House Salute to Gospel Music, Bush encountered the Gaither Vocal Band rehearsing in the East Room. He invited them to dinner. Instead of consulting "experts" on Third World development, Bush tapped U2 singer Bono as an adviser and ally on aiding sub-Saharan Africa. He invited Bono, a crusader for debt relief for poor countries, to two meetings in the Oval Office and rebutted a British reporter's sneering reference to him at a White House press conference in June 2005. "I admire him," the president said. "He is a man of depth and a great heart who cares deeply about the impoverished folks on the continent of Africa." Bono sent Bush a note of thanks for defending him.

Bush is neither an elitist nor a champion of elite opinion. He reflects the political views and cultural tastes of the vast majority of Americans who don't live along the East or West Coast. He's not a sophisticate and doesn't spend his discretionary time with sophisticates. As First Lady Laura Bush once said, she and the president didn't come to Washington to make new friends. And they haven't. They chiefly socialize with old friends, many of them Texans. Bush's view is that he and his aides are in Washington to do a job, then clear out of town. The day after the 2004 election, Bush reelection campaign strategist Matthew Dowd left a sign with the letters "GTT" on his office door. He had "gone to Texas" as quickly as possible to take a teaching post at the University of Texas and work as a political consultant. Bush will follow in 2009.

There are two types of presidents: those who govern and those who lead. A governing president performs all the duties assigned by the Constitution, deals with whatever issues or crises crop up during his term, and does little else. He's a caretaker. Richard Neustadt, in his seminal book *Presidential Power,* characterized such a president as essentially a clerk. Bush's father, George H. W. Bush, was a president who mainly governed. So was Dwight Eisenhower and, for most of his time in the White House, Bill Clinton.

Bush is a president who leads. "If we do not lead, people will suffer," the president told me in an interview I conducted specifically for this book. He controls the national agenda, uses his presidential powers to the fullest and then some, proposes far-reaching policies likely to change the way Americans live, reverses other long-standing policies, and is the foremost leader in world affairs. All the while, he courts controversy, provokes the press, and polarizes the country. The president doesn't worry about running the day-to-day activity of his own government; all he has to manage is the White House staff and individual cabinet secretaries.

His job, he told me, is to "stay out of minutiae, keep the big picture in mind, but also make sure that I know enough about what's going on to get the best information possible." To stress the point, during our interview in the Oval Office Bush called my attention to the rug; he had been surprised, he said, to learn that the first decision a president is expected to make is what color the rug should be. "I wasn't aware that presidents were rug designers," he told me. So he delegated the task—to Laura. Typical of his governing style, though, he gave a clear principle as guidance: he wanted the rug to express the view that an "optimistic person comes here." The rug she designed is sunrise yellow.

An approach like Bush's allows a president to drive policy initiatives, so long as he has a vision of where he wants to take the nation and the world. Bush, despite his wise-guy tendencies and cocky demeanor, is a visionary. So were Franklin D. Roosevelt and Ronald Reagan. They, too, were leaders, as controversial and polarizing as Bush.

To the political community—that amalgam of elected

officials, aides, advisers, consultants, lobbyists, bureaucrats, and journalists—Bush is a total surprise as president. In *A Charge to Keep*, his campaign book ghostwritten by adviser Karen Hughes and published in 1999, Bush foreshadowed his governing style and his reliance on his evangelical Christian faith. "I don't wait well," Bush said. He saw his job as chief executive as being "to set [the] agenda, to articulate the vision, and to lead." His interest "is not the means, it is the results." His faith, Bush said, "frees me. Frees me to make the decisions that others might not like. Frees me to try to do the right thing, even though it may not poll well. Frees me to enjoy life and not worry about what comes next." Few read the book and fewer still took it seriously. It was dismissed as superficial and self-serving.

Bush himself was seen as an intellectual bantamweight who would have difficulty governing after losing the popular vote to Al Gore in 2000 and winning the White House thanks to a 5–4 decision of the U.S. Supreme Court. He would have to govern as he had as governor of Texas. There, he had collaborated with Democratic lieutenant governor Bob Bullock and a Democratic legislature. In Washington, Democrats wanted Bush to function, in effect, as a national-unity president. Congressional Democrats would be partners in forging policies. It would be a degree of bipartisanship rarely seen in Washington. After all, Bush had said repeatedly in the 2000 campaign that he wanted to restore a tone of civility and cooperation to political relations in Washington. Republicans held only narrow majorities in both houses of Congress. And with a half-dozen moderate Republicans in the Senate always prepared to jump ship, Bush could not count on winning passage of his top priorities or confirmation of his appointees.

But the president quickly dashed expectations of two-party rule. He showed no signs of political weakness—quite the contrary. He stuck to his agenda of tax cuts, conservative judicial nominees, aid to faith-based programs, and education reform. Bush knew Democrats in Washington were not the same as Democrats in Austin. They were more liberal. If Democrats wavered, they faced the wrath of the liberal special-interest lobby, a collection of groups that represent—or at least claim to represent—organized labor, liberals, feminists, environmentalists, gays, foreign policy doves, and minorities. With their liberalism undiluted, Democrats on the Hill soon came to dislike the president. Bush found that he didn't like many of them either, particularly Tom Daschle, the Senate Democratic leader.

Only on his education reform package, dubbed No Child Left Behind, did the president find enough common ground for a compromise with Democrats. His partner was the Senate's preeminent liberal, Edward Kennedy. Soon after his inauguration, Bush had invited the senator and the entire Kennedy clan to the White House for a screening of *Thirteen Days*, a film about President John F. Kennedy and the 1962 Cuban missile crisis. Once the education bill was enacted, Bush and Kennedy took a two-day tour to tout their accomplishment. They joshed and teased like longtime pals. But the friendship soured as Bush pursued conservative policies that Kennedy loathed. Bush's idea of bipartisanship evolved into a congressional strategy of combining nearly all Republicans with a handful of Democrats. It worked. Ten Senate Democrats voted for the Bush tax cuts, providing the margin of victory for passage.

Democrats, the press, and the Washington establishment

all underestimated Bush. But that was hardly novel. The same thing had happened to Franklin D. Roosevelt and his cousin Theodore. The Washington community hopes that new presidents will be steeped in the intricacies of foreign and domestic policy, adept at political maneuvering, and high in brainpower; it undervalues the personal traits, character, and values of presidents.

There were great expectations for Clinton, a polished policy wonk, and Jimmy Carter, a detail man who instructed Cabinet members to read every single regulation that went out of their agencies. Both were failures, Clinton because of his indecision and undisciplined personal habits, Carter because of his counterproductive policies. Richard Nixon, with his political savvy and deep experience, also appeared destined for success before his paranoia doomed him.

FDR, TR, and Bush, on the other hand, were prematurely judged to fall short of presidential specifications. While still New York governor, Theodore Roosevelt had been dumped on William McKinley as his vice presidential running mate in 1900 by powerful New York Republicans who wanted him out of their hair. That was hardly an auspicious beginning for what became a dazzling career as a national leader. On the eve of FDR's inauguration as president, he was dismissed by columnist Walter Lippmann as "a pleasant man . . . without any important qualifications for office." Lippmann surely would have felt the same or worse about Bush.

What elite opinion missed about FDR, TR, and Bush was their temperament. Bush is actually a mixture of FDR and TR, with FDR's cool optimism and TR's pugnacity and determination. This combination strikes some, especially critics, as arrogance. A more charitable view is that Bush has the temperament of a self-assured Texas male. To those who insist he swaggers, Bush responds, "In Texas, we call it walking." Bush has a penchant for embracing big projects. He dismisses many issues as "small-ball" or "mini-ball"—not worth a president's time and attention. One of his favorite sayings is "We didn't come here to do school uniforms." It's a dig at Clinton, the master of the mini-proposal.

Bush regards himself as a problem solver. "If there is a problem," he told the *Wall Street Journal* as his second term began, "I have the responsibility to lay out potential solutions." And he told me when I interviewed him, "Every problem in the world comes here, which I like." When you add problem solving to a bias in favor of grand proposals, "you get George W. Bush," an aide said. And you also get a president who yearns to become what philosopher Sidney Hook called an "event-making leader," one who, by himself, changes the course of history. Being an "eventful leader" who merely handles the tribulations of his era skillfully is not on Bush's radar.

What Bush palpably lacks is a conservative governing temperament. "Conservatism is the right political philosophy," noted White House aide Peter Wehner, "but it can be the wrong political temperament." More often than not, liberals are activists and conservatives are not. Bush, however, is action-oriented. "For many years, conservatism was characterized by a suspicion and defensiveness toward the world," Wehner said in a little-noticed speech. "It was primarily a reactive political movement, which mitigated against boldness."

The most famous expression of this came from William F. Buckley Jr., who proclaimed in the inaugural issue of *National Review* that the role of conservatism is to "stand athwart history, yelling, 'Stop.'" Bush disagrees. We now live in an era when history must be shaped, not impeded, he believes. The role of a conservative president is "to be proactive, bold, energetic, and optimistic," Wehner said. And Bush is.

President Bush revealed his proactive tendencies after Hurricane Katrina devastated New Orleans and coastal Mississippi in the late summer of 2005. He quickly put the full resources of the federal government behind a costly recovery plan. It dwarfed the role of state and local governments and included a new antipoverty drive. "We will do whatever it takes," he said. "We will stay as long as it takes." Bush personally visited the damaged area eight times in the weeks after the storm. The price tag on his plan, estimated at more than $100 billion in federal spending, didn't faze him. If anything, he wished Washington had acted sooner and could do more. Many conservatives were appalled, likening the Bush effort to FDR's New Deal—to them, the epitome of Big Government overreach. They noted that a century earlier San Francisco had recovered in a few years from an earthquake and fire that destroyed the city and had done so without federal aid. The president and his aides were unsympathetic to their complaints.

Bush has set the bar high for his presidency. Like a student bent on improving his grade, he does the optional—the bigger the project, the better. Instead of relaxing and savoring a triumph, he moves ahead relentlessly. He went on, after overthrowing the Taliban and al Qaeda in Afghanistan, to target

Saddam Hussein. He ordered the invasion of Iraq against the wishes of France, Germany, China, Russia, and the United Nations, and once Saddam was defeated, Bush announced a worldwide drive for democracy. He won three tax cuts in his first term, yet called for sweeping tax reform in his second and set up a commission to design a simplified tax system. Bush devoted much of 2005 to campaigning for a complete overhaul of Social Security, rather than settling for modest reforms to shore up its finances. The day after he was reelected, he was already restless. He phoned speechwriter Michael Gerson and said the two of them had to get started on the inaugural address. It wouldn't be delivered for two and a half months.

As an insurgent, with few ties to Washington aside from an alliance with Republicans on Capitol Hill, Bush has found it easy to overturn major policies with scarcely a second thought. "As president, you get dealt a hand and you play it," he told me simply. In 2001 he casually announced that the administration would halt the practice of consulting the American Bar Association before going forward with judicial nominations, a practice that had given the ABA a virtual veto. Not used to such disrespectful treatment, the ABA cried foul, but it was too late.

The president later provoked worldwide protests when he formally withdrew the United States from the Kyoto global warming treaty. The environmental lobby in this country fumed, but Bush didn't flinch. The treaty had never been ratified and stood little chance of winning Senate approval. Though he didn't say so publicly, Bush is a dissenter on the theory of global warming. To the extent it's a problem, Bush believes it can be solved by technology. He avidly read Michael Crichton's 2004 novel *State of Fear*, whose villain falsifies scientific studies to justify draconian steps to curb global warming. Crichton himself has studied the issue extensively and concluded that global warming is an unproven theory and that the threat is vastly overstated. Early in 2005, political adviser Karl Rove arranged for Crichton to meet with Bush at the White House. They talked for an hour and were in near-total agreement. The visit was not made public for fear of outraging environmentalists all the more.

Bush was warned by the arms-control lobby that killing the Anti-Ballistic Missile Treaty with Russia would prompt a new arms race and perhaps a new Cold War. He was told the Russians were certain to react angrily. The president didn't believe any of it and wasn't deterred. When he pulled out of the treaty, the strongest language from Russian president Vladimir Putin was to call Bush's decision "a mistake." The predicted arms race hasn't occurred. Nor did a wave of testing of nuclear weapons occur after the president withdrew from the Comprehensive Test Ban Treaty, an unenforceable relic of the Cold War. In 2004, the White House announced that America would not accept the jurisdiction of the International Criminal Court in Brussels in any case. This made Europeans furious. But given the dangerous level of anti-Americanism awash in the world, the decision was sensible.

The boldest reversals in foreign policy affected the Middle East and terrorists. In his State of the Union address in 2002, Bush cast aside the seventy-year-old American policy of supporting stable but friendly dictatorships and autocracies in the Arab world. He advocated a movement toward democracy across the Middle East. To Bush's shock, the momentous policy change captured little attention. Instead, his denunciation of an "axis of evil" among Iraq, Iran, and North Korea crowded out other issues.

In policy discussions, Bush often poses fundamental questions. He once asked what the function of the Defense Department was. The purpose was to make sure the Pentagon was fulfilling its mission and not encroaching on other departments' turf. In the spring of 2002, he asked whether the Palestinians, with Yasser Arafat as their leader, constituted an entity with which Israel would ever feel comfortable reaching a final peace settlement. The answer was no. Bush decided this had to end. He sided with Israel's right to defend itself, which meant it could build a security fence along the West Bank and assassinate Palestinian terrorist leaders. As for the Palestinians, they had to create a democratic state prepared to negotiate honestly with Israel. Arafat? Since he would never accept a peace accord with Israel, the United States would have nothing more to do with him. Three years later, Arafat was dead, the Palestinians had a democratically elected government, the fence was nearly finished, the ranks of terrorist leaders had been thinned, and prospects for peace had brightened. And Arab states were lurching toward democracy.

Just as audacious was Bush's decision to sideline the national security policy of containment. It had been adopted after World War II to deal with the expansionist tendencies of the Soviet Union. By the late 1970s, it was not working, and President Reagan sponsored wars of national liberation in a few outlying Communist countries. But containment lingered as the official national security strategy even after the collapse of the Soviet Union. The terrorist attacks on the World Trade Center and the Pentagon on September 11, 2001, forced a change. Before then, Bush had barely scraped the surface of foreign policy. He had run for president almost solely on domestic issues. But he soon immersed himself in foreign affairs, and a policy of preemption emerged. Or more accurately, it was a policy of prevention. To prevent terrorist attacks, the United States would go after terrorists or after countries harboring terrorists on their home turf without waiting for them to attack America. This had already happened in the case of the Taliban government in Afghanistan and would happen again in Iraq in 2003. It was a forward-leaning strategy aimed primarily at uprooting terrorist cells of Islamic radicals all over the world. It seems to be working, at least in the continental United States. In the four years following 9/11, only two serious terrorist attacks occurred in non-Muslim countries: in Madrid in 2004 and London in 2005.

While running for president in 2000, Bush billed himself as a "different kind of Republican," which he is. In his acceptance speech at the Republican convention, he dipped into Catholic social thought to transform the Republican economic goal of prosperity into "prosperity with a purpose." The purpose was to extend prosperity to the poor, which had rarely been a Republican preoccupation. In the White House, Bush has proved to be a different kind of president, a risk taker with large plans and a willingness to accept criticism and hostility—and low approval ratings—as the price of boldness.

Now, with one four-year term under his belt, Bush turns

out to be a different kind of conservative, not just tempera-
mentally but philosophically as well. He calls himself a "compassionate conservative," but that doesn't come close to
encompassing the full range of his policies. Nor does the label
"big-government conservative" suffice. I'm actually responsible for that description, having coined the phrase in the early
1990s and applied it to Bush during his first term. The trouble
with that tag is it leaves the mistaken impression that he's not
really a conservative. But Bush is no libertarian or small-
government conservative either. Most Republicans, given their
belief in limited government, are one or the other of these.

Bush has a different take on government. The standard
conservative view is Jeffersonian: the less government, the
better off we'll be. The president pays lip service to limiting
the size and scope of the federal government, but it's not a top
Bush priority. In truth, his view of government is Hamilton-
ian: it's a valuable tool to achieve security, prosperity, and the
common good. His strategy is to use government as a means
to achieve conservative ends. Conservatives have long sought
to terminate the Department of Education, for example. Bush
is using it to require testing and accountability in public
schools. Sometimes Bush's goals don't seem quite so conservative. On immigration, Bush would curb the number of illegal
aliens in the country through a program of allowing a limited
number of immigrants to work here legally. Most conservatives prefer stiffer efforts to stop illegal immigrants at the border. Bush also rammed a Medicare prescription benefit through
Congress. For this, the only conservative rationales were the
creation of more health savings accounts, a free-market reform,

and the belief that a drug benefit passed by Democrats would be broader and more expensive. Liberals opposed the Bush bill, but only because Bush's name was on the legislation. In truth, it was the new entitlement they'd been dreaming about.

As a politician, Bush loves to smash conventional wisdom and destroy myths. It's generally agreed, for instance, that a new president has to reach out to the permanent Washington community for staffing his administration, for sage advice, and for social connections. Bush has ignored the inside-the-Beltway community without repercussions. Another piece of wisdom holds that a president must govern from the ideological center or he'll fail. Bush, at least in his first term, has governed successfully from the right. Also, presidents should never risk their standing by putting their prestige on the line in a midterm election. Bush did just that in 2002, and his party won House and Senate seats, even though the party in power traditionally loses seats in midterm elections. In 2004, Bush was warned by political experts that he couldn't both energize his conservative base and expand his electorate. But he did. At the same time, he erased the myth that a large voter turnout hurts Republicans.

In 2000 and 2004, Bush proved that Social Security is no longer the third rail of American politics. He trumpeted the idea of modernizing Social Security—by creating individual retirement accounts funded by payroll taxes—without suffering political death. Of course, actually enacting Social Security reform was a higher hurdle, one Bush found difficult to surmount in 2005.

Faced with another hurdle that year—namely, his first

nomination for the U.S. Supreme Court—Bush once again defied political expectations, not to mention political correctness. Instead of choosing a woman or a minority to replace Justice Sandra Day O'Connor—he could have named the first Hispanic justice, for instance—he selected a white male, John Roberts. And there was another wrinkle: Roberts is a conservative but not an unabashed ideological conservative of the sort the president has routinely nominated for lower federal courts. Some conservative interest groups pressed the White House to choose a nominee with an unequivocally conservative record, based perhaps on years of rulings as a federal appeals court judge. Bush rejected that advice. He believed Roberts, who had served only two years as an appeals judge, would have a better chance to win Senate confirmation.

Before Senate hearings on the Roberts nomination began, Chief Justice William Rehnquist died, creating a second vacancy. Bush quickly nominated Roberts for chief justice. His confidence was rewarded. Roberts was confirmed handily. For the still-vacant O'Connor seat, Bush pulled another surprise. He was expected to pick an identifiable conservative to replace the moderate O'Connor, shifting the balance on the court to the right. But Bush nominated the little-known Harriet Miers, the White House counsel. He insisted she was a judicial conservative. Many conservative politicians and commentators were outraged, however. Not only did they question whether she was a conservative, they also criticized her lack of credentials and experience. The result was a serious rift between the president and conservative activists. In fact, the outcry was so intense and Miers made such a weak impression in her private meetings with

Republican senators that she withdrew her name from consideration. Bush quickly nominated a certifiable conservative, Judge Samuel Alito of the U.S. Court of Appeals for the Third Circuit, to replace her. Conservative leaders responded enthusiastically.

For Bush, clashes with conservatives are inevitable. He pays little attention to the fine points of conservative dogma and has delegated the courting of conservative leaders and commentators to Karl Rove. His interest is solely in achieving conservative results. He nominated Miers, despite her lack of credentials, based on his belief that she would be a reliable conservative vote on the high court. His Katrina recovery plan aimed to turn the Gulf Coast into a hotbed of free enterprise and ownership. "I think this is a presidency," he told me, "that combines practical, hard-nosed policy, results-oriented policy, with a good healthy dose of idealism." He sought funds for faith-based groups because of their proven results in improving lives. Regarding his education policy, he said, "we have begun to cause reform to cascade by focusing on results." That emphasis on results is a "Republican principle," he told me. As much as they like conservative results, conservatives often disdain Bush's method of achieving them. More often than not, he relies on a bigger federal government and billions of taxpayer dollars. To conservatives, this is heresy. To Bush, it is practicality.

Given his rebel-in-chief style, President Bush is sometimes willing to take on fights with his conservative base, despite being a true (but unorthodox) conservative himself. Such fights challenge his ability to govern effectively, but he sees them as necessary to get what he considers important. A separate challenge came in October 2005, when Vice President Cheney's chief of staff, I. Lewis "Scooter" Libby, was indicted for perjury, false statements, and obstruction of justice in connection with special counsel Patrick Fitzgerald's probe into the leaking of CIA officer Valerie Plame's identity. Bush opponents had hoped Karl Rove and perhaps even Cheney himself would be indicted, too. They weren't (though Rove reportedly remained under investigation even after Libby was indicted). In any case, the Libby indictment alone wounded Bush. The president had a new task: engineering a political recovery from his early second-term slump.

FAITH AND LOYALTY

An overarching factor in the Bush presidency is his Christian faith. He is the first product of the modern evangelical movement, which blossomed in the 1980s, to reach the White House. This makes Bush an outsider in the largely secular political world. His faith is personal and intense. Bush prays off and on during the day, frequently in the Oval Office. He reads through the Bible every other year, and he also reads a daily devotional entitled *My Utmost for His Highest* by a British preacher, Oswald Chambers, who died nearly a century ago. His commitment to Jesus Christ as his personal savior makes temporal success in politics less important to him. Bush has often said that if he lost a presidential race, he could happily return to Texas. His life would not be diminished. There's a flip side: since politics is secondary, Bush feels free to take chances, ignore polls, expend his political capital, and go for broke on his agenda. When his presidency hit a rough patch in 2005, his faith kept him from getting despondent. One of his closest advisers said he was "irrepressible."

Though he has no religious litmus test, Bush has surrounded himself in the White House with fellow Christians. His four most influential advisers—Rove, Gerson, Cheney, and Secretary of State Condoleezza Rice—share his faith. Bush was very careful in selecting his inner circle. Prior to their first meeting, he knew exactly who Gerson was, including his religious background as an evangelical Christian and a graduate of Wheaton College, the Harvard of Christian colleges. "I've read your stuff," Bush began before Gerson had said a word. "I want you to move to Austin. I want you to work in the campaign." He said he wanted Gerson to write his acceptance speech and his inaugural address. Then Bush outlined why he wanted to be president. He was a compassionate conservative, fervent about domestic policy. He wanted to give people hope. "That was exactly what I wanted to hear," Gerson told me. "He was very persuasive about closing a deal." Gerson quickly packed up his wife and two kids and moved to Texas.

When Colin Powell resigned, Bush considered no one but Rice to replace him as secretary of state. After the 2000 campaign, Bush made call after call to Andy Card, a Washington lobbyist who had worked for the elder President Bush. Card was blasé about Bush's attention, but after several weeks called back. He was offered the job of White House chief of staff.

President Bush is a loyal man. He expects loyalty and gives it in return. When he lost the New Hampshire primary in 2000, his media advisers figured they'd be fired. "We're gone," Stuart Stevens said. But Bush told his aides that the loss was his fault and they weren't to blame. No one was fired. The day after winning reelection, Bush singled out Rove, the chief strategist in his four election victories (two for Texas governor, two for president), and called him "the architect" of his victory, a rare public tribute to a political operative. Bush kept Rove as a senior adviser even when Rove was under investigation in the CIA leak case, an indication of both loyalty and Bush's need for Rove's political guidance. Of course, as much as the president relies on Rove, he has occasionally interrupted a meeting at the White House to suggest that Rove take Barney, the Bush dog, outside.

A few weeks after his reelection, Bush ran into Larry Lindsey in the basement of the White House. Lindsey was Bush's chief economic adviser in the 2000 campaign and headed the National Economic Council in the White House before being eased out in 2003. Almost from the moment he began advising Bush in 1999, Lindsey had recommended a large tax cut. This was before the economy had been hit by the sharp stock market decline, the recession, or 9/11. His advice was radical, since tax cuts were seen as unnecessary, even harmful. When the president encountered Lindsey in the basement, he blurted, "You're the guy whose tax cuts won the election for me." Lindsey sheepishly suggested that other factors had contributed to Bush's victory. "No, we call it the Lindsey recovery around here," Bush said.

Lindsey was touched. As for Bush, he was grateful for bold—and prescient—advice that had served an insurgent president so well.

Chapter 2

The Outsider:
Bush and the Washington
Establishment

Y OU CAN LEARN A LOT about a city from its humor. And Washington is no exception.

John F. Kennedy, while still a young U.S. senator, described Washington as a city of "Northern charm and Southern efficiency." Ronald Reagan called Washington "an island surrounded on all sides by reality." Brent Scowcroft, the national security adviser to the first President Bush, characterized Washington as "a city where you don't have to worry about people stabbing you in the back—they'll stab you right in the front." A half-century ago, Senator Stuart Symington of Missouri dubbed Washington the only place "where the inmates run the asylum." What's the operating principle of the Washington press corps? It's simple: if you don't have anything nice to say, let's hear it. Then there's the story of Mayor Marion Barry, sarcastically referred to as Mayor for Life and once jailed on a cocaine conviction. Barry was said to have created a historic first when he was driven to his inauguration in a limousine whose license plates he had made.

The unflattering humor matches George W. Bush's negative view of Washington. Before he was elected president, he spent two stretches in D.C. He was miserable both times. In 1987, he moved to Washington with his family to help his father, then Ronald Reagan's vice president, run for president. Bush came specifically at the invitation of the elder Bush's campaign manager, Lee Atwater. He had been worried that Atwater and his team of political managers were more interested in making themselves look good than in getting his father elected president. "How do we know we can trust you?" Bush asked Atwater when they first met in 1986 at a family gathering at Camp David, the presidential retreat in Maryland. Following the meeting, Atwater buttonholed Bush. "If you're so worried about my loyalty, why don't you come to Washington and help me with the campaign?" Atwater said. "That way if there's a problem, you'll be there to solve it." Bush agreed and stayed through his father's victory over Democrat Michael Dukakis in November 1988. Four years later, when his father sought reelection, Bush was a frequent visitor to Washington to check on the campaign.

He grew to loathe almost everything about Washington. Though his father, born and bred in New England, moved with ease in Washington circles, Bush didn't, and didn't want to. He made few friends there. Bush had spent most of his life in Texas and exemplified the state's plain-spoken, straightforward style. He found people in Washington, in and out of government, to be self-important, obsequious, and quite different from folks outside the Beltway. Bush felt they were obsessed with their status as leaders or opinion makers or prominent lobbyists or socialites or former something-or-others. He hated the culture of Washington, particularly the notion of political and even social life in the city as a zero-sum game where there's a loser for every winner. He didn't see politics that way, much less social gatherings.

He still doesn't. As president, Bush has found that "the zero-sum attitude . . . is pervasive on Capitol Hill in many ways," he told me. The vote on the Central America Free Trade Agreement (CAFTA) in July 2005, with Democrats eager to deal Bush a politically harmful defeat, was a "classic example," he said. CAFTA won narrowly.

Bush also developed a powerful dislike for the national press corps. In Washington, many reporters and columnists circulate among the city's elite. They reminded Bush of the liberal students he detested in his years at Yale. He regarded them as condescending know-it-alls. Bush was particularly contemptuous of *Time* Washington bureau chief Strobe Talbott, a fellow Yalie. In Washington, he made fun of Talbott's full name, Nelson Strobridge Talbott, by dragging out the pronunciation. Talbott later left journalism and served in the Clinton administration before becoming president of the Brookings Institution, Washington's premier liberal think tank.

As unpleasant as Bush found Washington in 1987 and 1988, his experience in 1992 was worse. He spent much of this time asking second-level operatives how his father's campaign was doing. He figured they had the best grasp of the question. Not well, they told him. Bush felt the principals in the campaign's hierarchy were incompetent or halfhearted. And he believed several of them bailed out on his father well before election day.

Among others, he soured on James A. Baker III, then White House chief of staff and one of his father's closest friends. Bush wound up so disillusioned he barred anyone from the 1992 campaign from a role in his own presidential campaign in 2000. But when the 2000 race ended without a winner, he summoned Baker to direct his effort in the thirty-six-day recount in Florida. His grudge notwithstanding, he knew Baker was politically crafty and ruthlessly efficient. Bush ultimately appointed two of Baker's associates to positions in his new administration: Robert Zoellick as special trade representative and John Bolton as undersecretary of state for arms control and international security and then as ambassador to the United Nations. Baker, looking for a conservative aide, had hired Bolton years earlier to his staff at the Reagan White House on the recommendation of David Keene, now head of the American Conservative Union.

Bush adviser Karl Rove has an all-purpose explanation for the president's aversion to the habits of Washington. It's "M and M," shorthand for Midland, Texas, where Bush grew up, and Methodism, the workingman's Protestant denomination. Midland taught Bush small-town values like loyalty and keeping your promises, which are often honored in the breach in Washington. Methodism, spread among the poor and middle-class in eighteenth-century England by John Wesley, stresses such traits as morality, responsibility, and character.

Bush follows the un-Washington regimen of early to bed, early to rise, going to bed at 9:30 P.M. and getting up at 5:30 A.M. "He's not hanging out at the Kennedy Center," Mark McKinnon, Bush's chief media consultant in 2000 and 2004, told me. At the state dinner for the prime minister of India in July 2005, he cut off the postmeal entertainment after five songs by the Preservation Hall Band. "At least two of us" are going to bed, he said, speaking for himself and the first lady. Then, looking at the Indian leader and his wife, Bush said, "Four of us." And the Bushes departed for their bedroom upstairs at the White House. It was a few minutes before 10 P.M.

"I'm really not a part of the Washington society," the president told me. "I've got a lot to do. We're at war and I've got a lot of reading to do in the evening when they drop papers off and the president gives a lot of speeches." Bush acknowledged that there's been "a little blowback" from this. "They think I'm disrespecting people, but this is the way it is. I'm not a night owl. I don't really care that much for the glitterati."

McKinnon, who spends two days a week in Washington, has closely watched the president rub up against the city and its political culture. Bush has avoided the temptations of Washington, he says. "It's easy to get sucked into the Washington mind-set and echo chamber," which lead nearly everyone in town "to swarm like moths to whatever may be the issue of the day." But Bush hasn't been. He's "stayed aloof from D.C.," McKinnon commented, and this has advantages. "It's very healthy. It allows him to be bold, to throw deep, and to defy the conventional wisdom. He's not persuaded by the chorus of Washington. He's just immune to it. He'll rely on his own instincts."

Bush puts Washington in a special category: his job site. As Vice President Dick Cheney told me, "This is where you come to work." The president doesn't find his time in Washington to be relaxing—ever. "When he wants to relax, he goes home to Texas," Cheney said. Hence, he often goes to his ranch in Crawford, outside Waco. An invitation to visit him there has become a symbol of respect for foreign leaders.

When Bush encountered Larry Lindsey, his former chief economic adviser, in the basement of the White House after his reelection, he not only praised Lindsey for his advice but also hugged him. The fact was, when Bush had fired Lindsey in 2003, Treasury Secretary Paul O'Neill had been the real target. Lindsey was fired at the same time as O'Neill merely for show—a demonstration of White House concern over a struggling economy. He was a scapegoat. "That's more typical of Washington than it was of Bush," Lindsey told me. And no doubt Bush felt ashamed for indulging, just that once, in the ways of Washington.

THE POPULIST VS. THE ELITIST

Given his values, Bush was bound to form a distinctly unfavorable opinion of the vast army of unofficial Republican advisers ensconced in Washington's teeming law firms, trade groups, and lobbying outfits. They had stayed in Washington after working on Capitol Hill, in earlier Republican administrations, or as party apparatchiks. Now they'd become part of the permanent Washington establishment. It was inevitable that Bush would despise them. They had become elitists. Bush is a populist.

Populism had its day in Washington. Southerners controlled Congress and dominated Washington for the first half of the twentieth century. Their goals were simple: bring federal largesse to their states and block racial integration. No doubt Bush would have gotten along swimmingly with them except on racial issues, just as he did with conservative Texas Democrats when he was governor.

But the power of Southern Democrats eroded after World War II, and by the time John F. Kennedy was elected president in 1960, their day was over. Kennedy, with his attraction to Ivy League academics and young liberal idealists, ushered in the modern era in Washington. The reputation of Washington as a sleepy Southern town with bad restaurants and minimal nightlife faded. Washington became the glamorous city on the Potomac in which liberals were brimming with new ideas while conservatives were brain-dead. Democrats, freed from their Southern yoke, enacted nearly every piece of liberal legislation proposed since the New Deal in the 1930s, plus a host of freshly minted measures. And the power of Washington grew as the size and scope of the federal government mushroomed and its influence across the country deepened.

With hardly anyone taking note, a demographic trend appeared that would shape the future of Washington, hastening the advent of a political culture unique to the nation's capital and aloof from most of America. Until the 1960s, those who worked in Congress or the White House or a cabinet department or a regulatory agency returned home when their government employment ended. There was no financial incentive to stay. Washington's private sector was relatively small, and high-paying jobs were scarce. But the New Deal, World War II, the New Frontier, and the Great Society gradually changed the city. Since the government now intervened in all aspects of business, commerce, and public life, corporations and industries suddenly realized they needed full-time assistance in Washington. So did pressure groups. In a word, they needed lobbyists. Every large company, every industrial sector, every major ideological group, indeed every state government, and virtually every foreign government—together they shared a fear of leaving their fortunes to the whims of Washington.

Supply soon followed demand. Washington law firms metastasized, and law firms based in New York, Cleveland, Chicago, Houston, Dallas, Los Angeles, and every other large city in America deployed lawyers in Washington. Their job was not primarily to litigate but to lobby. Hundreds of specialized lobbying and public relations firms opened. Trade groups set up shop. Labor unions relocated to Washington. Political consultants made Washington their home base. The result was thousands of lucrative jobs. A retiring congressman or a staff lawyer for the House Ways and Means Committee or a White House assistant discovered that his talents were more valuable in Washington than back in his home state. For one thing, the pay was better in Washington. Marty Franks, a White House aide to President Carter and later executive director of the Democratic Congressional Campaign Committee, left in the 1980s to work for a Midwest company, only to find that the skills he'd honed in Washington weren't as useful outside the Beltway. He returned to Washington and became chief lobbyist for CBS. Meanwhile, think tanks proliferated, some with perches for well-known political figures with lavish pay and little serious work. The result: the tide of emigrants from Washington slowed as more and more people made the city their permanent home.

The trend quickly became a pattern, the pattern a rule: the majority of those who take political jobs in Washington never leave. By the 1980s, Washington had emerged as a world-class city in wealth and sophistication and the trappings of luxury. Aside from government, though, much of Washington amounts to a parasite culture. The tangible work product of Washington's private sector often consists of nothing more than paper. The city specializes in political connections, talk, informed gossip, and endless meetings. A lobbyist who once a decade gets a single provision in a tax bill that helps a client is considered successful. The pay scale has ratcheted upward to the point where the relationship between effort and reward is badly misaligned. Yet the conceit of Washingtonians is that they are indispensable to the smooth functioning of the country. This conceit contributed to George W. Bush's dislike of Washington, which hardened into a strong prejudice during his two episodes as campaign adviser to his father.

Bush didn't care much for the Washington political establishment either. Contrary to the doubters, the establishment does exist. It acts like a Greek chorus, voicing opinions from the sidelines. It consists of lobbyists and lawyers and consultants, leftovers from Congress and earlier administrations, the permanent bureaucracy at prestige departments (State, Justice, Treasury), trade group representatives and think tank fellows, Capitol Hill staffers (chiefly Democrats), and the media—especially the media. The establishment carries weight. It affects the mood in Washington and shapes the zeitgeist. It's become more Republican with so many officials of the Reagan and elder Bush administrations hanging around. But it's still center-left ideologically. Its temperament is reactionary. The establishment furiously opposes Bush-style conservative change that would alter or reverse liberal programs or policies of the past seventy-plus years. But what infuriates establishment types the most is that Bush ignores them.

The establishment operates through images, buzz, and leaks. In the 1980s, it clung to the image of Reagan as a dope or, in the words of establishment superlawyer Clark Clifford, an "amiable dunce." The establishment image of the Bush White House has Dick Cheney and Karl Rove in charge, not the president. Bush's ardent Christian faith is a special annoyance and thus a constant source of buzz. Unlike mere gossip, buzz is supposed to contain at least a kernel of real information. But it often doesn't. When Bush ordered the invasion of Iraq in 2003, buzz widely repeated inside the establishment faulted him not only for believing that God had ordered him to invade but for actually telling people that. This buzz was untrue on both counts.

Leaks are the most cunning tactic of the establishment. Since the permanent bureaucracy is part of the Bush administration, a highly critical leak by a Bush-hating official at the State Department can be attributed to a "senior Bush administration official." This implies that the leaker is a Bush appointee and bolsters the credibility of the leak. There have been many such leaks on Iraq. On political matters, nearly every onetime Republican bigwig in Washington has offered his opinion to Bush, his campaign staff, the Republican National Committee, or someone who works for the president. That person, in divulging hostile information about the president, becomes "a Bush adviser" for purposes of identification. This creates the false impression of discontent among Bush advisers, a group remarkable for its unity. In one sense, leaks work: they exasperate Bush.

The media—top reporters, columnists, TV commentators—are the shock troops of the establishment. They echo establishment thinking. To put it mildly, Bush does not enjoy the company of journalists. In fact, no president has since Gerald Ford, who served from 1974 to 1977. Ford had made friends with a half-dozen reporters during his years in the House of Representatives and as vice president. Carter had favorites in the Washington press corps, but no friends. Reagan scarcely knew the names of reporters. According to an establishment myth, the elder Bush invited Brit Hume, then of ABC and now a Fox News anchor, to play tennis with him on the White House courts. In truth, that never happened. Clinton was close to a number of political writers until he became president, when most of them turned on him.

The media voice of the establishment is the *Washington Post*. This is a problem for Bush and his aides for two reasons. First, the *Post*'s White House reporters have been sharply critical of Bush and his presidency. And second, everyone in Washington reads the paper. A classic example of the establishment speaking was a story on the *Post*'s front page in the early days of the war in Iraq in late March 2003. At the time, critics claimed the war was going poorly. The story said that "former senior Republican government officials and party leaders" were waging a "behind-the-scenes effort" to persuade Bush he'd gotten "bum advice" on Iraq. Those involved were obviously not former Bush officials, and it was unclear if the "party leaders" were official or unofficial, former or current. In any event, they lacked direct influence on the president, and their "effort" never got off the ground. Within days American troops poured into Baghdad and Saddam Hussein's regime collapsed.

A journalistic device of the *Post* is to attribute criticism of Bush or his policies to "some critics," a synonym for the Washington establishment. "Some critics," for instance, said Bush was too accommodating to Russian president Vladimir Putin when they met in February 2005. And "some critics" said Bush's second inaugural speech stressing democracy was a "potentially mistaken expression of U.S. foreign policy."

Stubborn and standoffish, Bush has seldom courted the press—quite the contrary. At a Dallas restaurant in 1986, Bush confronted Al Hunt, then Washington bureau chief of the *Wall Street Journal.* Hunt had predicted that Bush's father would lose the 1988 Republican presidential nomination to Jack Kemp. Bush, who had been drinking, said threateningly, "I will never forget what you wrote." Years later, Bush apologized to Hunt, now with Bloomberg News. There's an epilogue to the story. Presidents regularly attend the annual dinner in Washington of the Gridiron Club, an elite group of print reporters. But when Bush declined in 2004, reporters figured it was because he would have had to sit for the entire evening next to the club's president—Hunt.

Bush does respect at least one Washington reporter, Tom DeFrank, the D.C. bureau chief of the *New York Daily News*. DeFrank is a Texan and a graduate of Texas A&M. In 1987, the elder Bush barred aides from talking to *Newsweek* after the magazine published a cover story on him and the "wimp factor." Nonetheless, Bush's father told him it was fine to talk to DeFrank, then a *Newsweek* reporter. They met secretly throughout 1988 and then in 1992.

Bush prefers to needle the press. In his first presidential campaign, he famously told reporters, "I don't read half of what you write." One reporter answered, "We don't listen to half of what you say." Bush got the last word, saying this explained the poor quality of their reporting. As president, Bush mocked NBC correspondent David Gregory when he asked a question in French at a joint press conference in Paris with Bush and French president Jacques Chirac. Bush insists he barely reads the newspapers and watches little TV, relying instead on aides to inform him of anything noteworthy in the news. Actually, he looks at four newspapers in the morning, starting with the conservative *Washington Times*, and receives the *Dallas Morning News* later in the day, concentrating on its sports section. The president is backstopped by his wife, Laura, who reads the newspapers thoroughly.

TEXANS, NOT TUXES

By the end of Bush's first term, it was clear that he wanted little to do with the Washington establishment. He had practiced his can't-be-bothered approach from the moment he arrived in Washington in 2001. An earlier Republican outsider, Ronald Reagan, had handled things differently. When he landed in Washington in 1980 as president-elect, Reagan quickly got in the establishment's good graces, despite his conservative views and the anti-Washington rhetoric for which he'd become famous. Katherine Graham, the publisher of the *Washington Post*, invited him to a welcome-to-Washington party at her Georgetown mansion. Reagan and his wife, Nancy, gladly accepted, signaling their desire to have cordial relations with elite Washington. Nancy, with her blue-state opinions and scorn for her husband's unpolished supporters, became the perfect emissary to the establishment.

Twenty years later, Bush had no interest in a social powwow with establishment stalwarts. His administration's closest thing to an ambassador to the Washington establishment was Colin Powell. But Powell was too busy as secretary of state to socialize, and besides, he left the Bush administration early in 2005.

Bush has made a fetish out of getting out of Washington whenever possible. As Cheney indicated, the president treats Washington as the workplace to which he commutes. In his first four-year term, he spent more than a third of his time at Camp David or his Crawford ranch. He held amazingly few state dinners—a mere four in four years. These are the social events to which establishment figures relish an invitation. If they are invited, their names appear the next day in the widely read fine print in the Style section of the *Washington Post*. Laura Bush occasionally eats lunch with friends in Washington restaurants. But the president rarely eats out, and his early-to-bed discipline rules out heavy socializing. On the evening of his second inauguration, Bush and his wife raced through appearances at nine balls, returning to the White House in time to meet Bush's normal bedtime. During the Christmas season, the White House has nightly parties. The singing of carols is limited so Bush can depart early for bed.

The president has made little effort to make new friends in Washington, and the unsurprising result is that he hasn't made many. Whenever possible, he skips banquets or dinners that presidents normally attend. In 2005, he dispatched Cheney as his surrogate at the Radio and TV Correspondents' Dinner. Bush, who rarely puts on formal wear, made one bow to the establishment when he showed up in a tuxedo at the British Embassy for a party honoring his new secretary of state, Condoleezza Rice, a woman the president regards as a sister. "One tux a term," a White House official told me. "That's our idea of outreach to the Washington community."

In effect, Bush has thumbed his nose at Washington. "A lot of it is worth thumbing your nose at," Stephen Hess, a Brookings Institution scholar on the presidency and an aide in the Eisenhower White House, told me. "There's a lot of phoniness here." Most presidents try to accommodate Washington. When Carter was in political trouble in 1979, he retreated to Camp David and called in waves of Washington establishment figures for consultation. Afterward, he announced that neither he nor Washington was the source of America's problems; the American people were. Reagan relied on Nancy to mollify the establishment. The elder Bush was a member in good standing, and besides, he promised a "kinder, gentler" administration more in sync with Washington's predilections. Clinton was respectful of the establishment, except the press. Nixon and Johnson? They suffered from being constantly compared with their predecessor, Kennedy. JFK was the peerless establishment favorite—attractive, liberal, and urbane.

Bush's distaste for Washington is not entirely visceral. Washington has firmly held attitudes about what's required to get along in the city, plus a set of political opinions as well. Bush disagrees across the board. Washington's top ten attitudes start with the notion that newcomers must reach out to the local political community for advice and appointees to high positions. Bush prefers Texans. And when he has tapped Washington veterans, they've often been outcasts bent on shaking up institutions revered by the establishment. At the outset of his second term, he nominated Paul Wolfowitz, who strongly influenced Bush's Iraq and Middle East policies, to run the World Bank. Washington frowned. Then the president picked Bolton, James Baker's man, as ambassador to the United Nations, an institution Bolton had noisily attacked. Washington fumed.

Next on the list of attitudes is the one holding that it's okay to campaign against or criticize Washington so long as you don't believe what you're saying. In Bush's case, he believes it. A third attitude is that it's a serious faux pas to spurn the social whirl in Washington. Those who do so are seen as rednecks, social misfits, or religious zealots.

Two Washington attitudes deal specifically with religion. One is that religious faith should never be a significant part of anyone's thinking on politics or policy. Bush, to the contrary, has aggressively sought (and won) the support of evangelical Christians. And one of his major domestic programs is a faith-based initiative aimed at using religious groups to aid the poor, homeless, addicted, and dysfunctional. "I'm a positive result from a faith-based initiative," Bush told me, "albeit it was a one-person faith-based program in the form of Billy Graham, who inspired me to get back into the Good Book and by doing so I began to examine my own habits and eventually quit drinking." The other attitude so common to Washington is that Sunday mornings aren't for church but for watching TV interview shows like *Meet the Press* and *Fox News Sunday*. Bush usually attends church. Even when he doesn't, he never watches the Sunday shows.

Two more attitudes involve the expected role of conservatives. Conservatives who move left as they linger in Washington are "growing" and maturing and deserve respect. Liberals who move right are either pandering or selling out. Washington relishes political compromise, and it's the obligation of conservatives to do most of the compromising. As a conservative, Bush balks at both of these notions.

And he is diametrically opposed to the three most widely shared attitudes in Washington. The belief that the press is usually right—that's the mainstream press—clashes with what

Bush has experienced in his political career. "He's not reading the *New York Times* for advice," a senior Bush aide told me. In addition, in a White House–centric town, the buzz is always about who is telling the president what to do, for the conventional view in Washington is that conservative Republican presidents are, simply put, dumb. Bush, understandably, believes he makes up his own mind. The foremost attitude is that Washington knows best. To Bush, this is the ultimate expression of Washington's vanity and self-importance. In 2000, Bush was asked what he'd do if he lost the election and didn't get to Washington. "Go fishing," he said, making it sound like a quite satisfactory alternative.

THE TEN COMMANDMENTS, WASHINGTON-STYLE

Washington's articles of political faith are no less repugnant to Bush than the get-along attitudes. They reflect a center-left ideology dominant since the 1930s. It's a softer brand of liberalism than that of the 1960s and 1970s, but liberalism nonetheless. What's amazing is that liberalism has managed to survive in Washington through eras of strong conservative presidents like Reagan and Bush and episodes of conservative control of Congress—including the past decade. A thread that runs through the city's liberal faith is that what is said and done in Washington is more significant and certainly more benign than what occurs outside the city. And the city in this case is not the Washington metropolitan area inside the capital Beltway, which consists mostly of suburbs, or even the smaller District of Columbia part. The real city is political Washington. A circle around this area, an Inner Beltway, would encompass the White House, Foggy Bottom, Capitol Hill, Georgetown, downtown Washington, embassy row, the K Street corridor famous for its lobbyists, the Pentagon, and the section of Alexandria, Virginia, that houses lobbyists and Republican political consultants. This is where the political community works. This is where Bush does not feel at home.

The ten commandments of the Washington political creed begin with a belief that the issue of abortion should be kept out of politics and policy. Bush, on the contrary, champions a "culture of life" and has signed three bills curbing abortions and promoted others. The next article proclaims that judges know best, except those who insist on a close reading of the laws and the Constitution. The president has battled with congressional Democrats over his nomination of federal appeals judges who would stick to a close reading. And his first Supreme Court nominee, John Roberts, was of the same ilk.

Then come the foreign and defense policy commandments that Washington favors and Bush doesn't. In foreign affairs, the Washington wisdom holds that multilateralism trumps unilateralism and that when there's a multilateral coalition operating, it should determine the mission, not the other way around. Bush, however, is on board with the view of his defense secretary, Donald Rumsfeld, that the mission should determine the coalition, as it did in Afghanistan and Iraq. Washington punctuated its love affair with multilateralism in the spring of 2005 when a prominent establishment couple, former *Washington Post* editor Ben Bradlee and wife Sally Quinn, held a party at their home to honor Kofi Annan, the United Nations secretary general. This was a finger in the eye to Bush. Annan, who had insisted the war in Iraq was illegal, was a frequent critic of Bush's foreign policy.

Another commandment holds that in foreign policy disputes with Europeans, the European position is invariably saner, more sophisticated, and more advanced than the popular American view. Bush has pungently expressed his disgust with this notion. When British prime minister Tony Blair suggested that French president Jacques Chirac was worth talking to about a specific issue, Bush said forget it. Chirac is "an asshole," he declared.

Two articles deal directly with the military. One says that American military force should rarely be used, but when it must, it should be to join or aid allies or to serve a social cause, not American interests. This view countenances Clinton's bombing of Serbia but not Bush's invasion of Iraq. The president's strategy of preemption—attacking enemies before they attack America or Americans—would be problematic if he subscribed to this limit on military force. The other military dictum stipulates that the most important part of any military operation is the exit strategy, unless it's a humanitarian mission. During the Iraq War and its aftermath, non-Bush Washington hollered repeatedly for an announced exit strategy. Bush demurred, arguing that a declared plan for getting out could only prolong a conflict and encourage the enemy to hang tight. With the success of the Iraqi election, Bush was vindicated.

The Washington political dogma elevates the importance of Washington. How best to solve problems? Easy. Nearly every problem in America can be solved by legislation, regulation, or more federal spending, all carried out in Washington. If a program isn't working, it's because it is underfunded. Bush isn't philosophically or practically averse to legislating and spending. But he tilts in favor of programs that give individuals freedom over how they spend government subsidies or their own money.

One article of Washington faith is obvious and self-serving: federal power is preferable to state power. Here, Bush is not a conventional conservative. He's favorably disposed to federal power in education and health care. The crowning Washington belief is that the first job of the economy is to finance the government. This is an idea that makes perfect sense to Washington lifers, but to no one else, including Bush. He believes the first job of government, after keeping the American people secure, is to nurture economic conditions that assure prosperity. For Bush, it means that government intervention in the economy should be proscribed, not prescribed.

There's one more article of faith. It sides with Washington's most potent interest group, the press, over its next most powerful, government. It posits that secrecy in government is almost always a conspiracy against the press, since there are few legitimate government secrets. And the press accuses Bush of leading the most secretive administration in recent memory. Bush takes the accusation as a compliment. Reporters have complained bitterly about the paucity of information and helpful sources, and they have taken their frustration out on the White House press office, especially by hectoring Bush's second press secretary, Scott McClellan, at daily briefings.

Washington has its seductions. Life in Washington is easier for a president if he lightens up and accommodates a handful of the establishment's attitudes and political views. His press coverage is kinder. The buzz about him is nicer. His image changes from intolerant right-winger to open-minded, flexible conservative. Protest demonstrations fizzle or cease. Accept the parameters and boundaries set by Washington, and the presidency is a piece of cake.

But there's a trade-off. Accepting the strictures of Washington brings admiration and respect now but nothing later— no serious change, no rerouting of the course of history, no breakthroughs that improve lives everywhere. So Bush has not only resisted the temptations of Washington; he's blotted them out. In sociological terms, he's an inner-directed man in an other-directed town. His focus is on giving Americans more power over their own lives and wealth and changing the way the world is governed. It's a revolutionary vision that may exceed Bush's power to achieve it. But if he fails, it won't be because he fell victim to the blandishments of Washington.

Chapter 3

Strike the Hole, Strike the Rancher: The Bush Revolution in Foreign Policy

Tony Blair, the British prime minister, talked amicably to President Bush by phone on election day, November 2, 2004. But he went to bed thinking that Senator John Kerry, Bush's Democratic challenger, had won the presidential election. London is five hours ahead of Washington, and all Blair knew was the result of early exit polls showing Kerry in a romp over Bush. So Blair instructed his aides to wake him at 3 A.M. so he could call Kerry once his victory was assured. But they didn't wake him. And when he got up later, Blair was told that Bush had been reelected.

He was no doubt relieved. Though he never publicly stated a preference in the American presidential race, he and Bush had forged an alliance on Iraq and terrorism, as well as an unexpectedly close friendship. The long-standing special relationship between England and the United States became every bit as strong as it had been in the 1980s, when Ronald Reagan was president and Margaret Thatcher was prime minister. The Bush-Blair alliance, however, is more consequential.

Bush needs Blair, and vice versa. For Bush, the tight partnership is an essential ingredient of his new foreign policy in the aftermath of the terrorist attacks of September 11, 2001, on the World Trade Center and the Pentagon. It is a world-changing policy crafted mostly by Bush himself, not his advisers. And it is a policy that has significantly strengthened America's strategic position in the world.

What made Blair's close association with Bush slightly shocking was the warm relationship he'd had with Bush's predecessor, Bill Clinton, who is as different from Bush as a politician could be. Blair regarded Clinton as the premier politician of the late twentieth century, a quick study who could master any issue almost instantly. He and Clinton also had similar political interests. They both liked to ruminate, publicly and in their private conversations, about a "third way" for center-left leaders to govern, a way that jettisoned both socialism and old-fashioned liberalism without winding up by embracing conservatism.

With Bush, the relationship was less chummy but more practical. Bush had the one trait that Blair found lacking in Clinton: reliability. Clinton talked big, but Blair never knew if he would back up his words with actions. With Bush, he knew. Blair told associates that Bush was "very bright," would get to the nub of an issue quickly and decisively, and would do what he said he would do. Blair felt he could trust Bush. And as a Christian, he wasn't turned off by Bush's religiosity. They occasionally prayed together.

That Blair was so attracted to Bush, even to the point of eagerly signing up for the unpopular war in Iraq, shouldn't have been surprising for two other reasons. First, Blair believed that Great Britain's future in the world was inextricably tied to its relationship with America, and thus he felt that nurturing the special relationship with the United States was his first obligation as prime minister. He saw himself as the bridge between America and Europe, which enhanced his influence in both places. (He also found, to his delight, that he and Bush shared a loathing for French president Jacques Chirac.) Second, Blair advocated the same interventionist principles as Bush. The British prime minister became even more outspoken on these points after the terrorist bombings of the London subway on July 7, 2005, but in fact he was advocating this view even before Bush himself was.

In addition to championing intervention in Kosovo in the 1990s, Blair spelled out his views in a little-noticed speech in Chicago in 1999. "The most pressing foreign policy problem we face is to identify the circumstances in which we should get actively involved in other people's conflict," Blair said then. The principle of noninterference must be qualified, he noted. "War is an imperfect instrument for righting humanitarian distress, but armed force is sometimes the only means of dealing with dictators. . . . In the past we talked too much about exit strategies. But having made a commitment to stay, we cannot simply walk away once the fight is over. Better to stay with moderate numbers of troops than return for repeat performances with large numbers." In the speech, Blair mentioned Iraqi dictator Saddam Hussein by name. He also disputed the idea that a leader must choose between a moral foreign policy promoting freedom and one pursuing national interests. "If we can establish and spread the values of liberty, the rule of law, human rights, and an open society, then that is in our national interests, too," Blair said. This was prescient. It was a theme of Bush's second inaugural address in 2005.

At a time when Blair was a full-throated foreign policy idealist, Bush stressed domestic policy. Foreign affairs were tangential to his presidential campaign in 1999 and 2000. Bush didn't fall into either of the two foreign policy camps, idealist or realist. Idealists have a simple set of beliefs. They champion liberty, democracy, and free markets—and regime change if necessary to achieve them. They are moralists. What realists favor is more complicated. They put a high premium on stability among nations and view democracy and even elections as ill-suited for much of the world. They have a soft spot for pro-American autocrats. Realists are skeptical of America's ability to change the world. Given that perspective, America should pursue its narrow interests, not grandiose schemes for improving the world.

Realism has a long tradition among Republican leaders. Bush's own father, President George H. W. Bush, and his father's national security adviser, Brent Scowcroft, and secretary of state, James A. Baker III, were all realists. President Richard Nixon was the foremost American realist. His secretary of state, Henry Kissinger, said that after many talks he "came to understand his subtle circumlocutions better. I learned that to Nixon words were like billiard balls. What mattered was not the initial impact but the carom." Columnist Charles Krauthammer has dubbed the realist view as the "billiard ball theory" of foreign affairs. The important thing is how the balls—a metaphor for powerful nations—play off one another. Idealists believe what the balls represent, their actual content, is paramount. Their goal is more balls associated with democracy and the other lofty principles of freedom.

The Bush foreign policy of 1999 and 2000, what there was of it, was not his own. At the time, he was a student of his advisers, particularly Condoleezza Rice, then provost at Stanford University. An appointee to the first President Bush's National Security Council, Rice was a protégé of Scowcroft, the unswerving realist. In George W. Bush's first major foreign policy speech, delivered at the Reagan Library in California in late 1999, he sounded like Rice. His views reflected those she expressed in a *Foreign Affairs* article published a few weeks later. Where she criticized the Clinton administration's deployment of troops on humanitarian missions to Haiti and Kosovo, Bush said the American military is not the answer "to every difficult foreign policy situation." Where Rice wrote, "America's pursuit of the national interest will create conditions that promote freedom, free markets, and peace," Bush said his "great and guiding goal" was to achieve "generations of democratic peace . . . by concentrating on enduring national interests." In other words, both said realist means would eventually produce idealist ends. Idealists see it the other way around: pursuing democracy promotes a nation's interests. The real clue that the speech was more Rice than Bush was its emphasis on Russia. Rice is a Russia specialist, and her *Foreign Affairs* treatise had the same emphasis.

Despite Rice's guidance—and she would become national security adviser in Bush's first term—it was unclear what exact shape a Bush foreign policy would take. Bush's summary of his views was confusing. He endorsed "idealism without illusions, confidence without conceit, realism in the service of American ideals." Any modern president could have said the same. It meant nothing.

Even before 9/11, Bush showed signs that he did not fully embrace the realist vision. His instinct was to take America's enemies for what they were, thugs and killers, and not as worthy partners in hopeful negotiations. In *Rise of the Vulcans*, James Mann's insightful book about the hard-liners advising Bush, an aide tells of an outburst by the president in a foreign policy discussion in the early months of his administration, pre-9/11. Bush interrupted to focus on one country's leaders. "We're talking about them as though they were members of the Chevy Chase Country Club," he said. "What are they really like? . . . How brutal are these people?"

The 9/11 assault by al Qaeda terrorists changed Bush's approach to foreign policy in important ways. Within hours of the attacks, Bush was already fashioning a new policy. It was a Bush policy, not the work of his advisers. He was no longer the attentive student. Now he was the policy maker. And the president was soon finding new allies and shedding old ones. National Security Adviser Rice, Vice President Cheney, Defense Secretary Donald Rumsfeld, Secretary of State Colin Powell—they followed their leader.

The terrorist attacks influenced Bush the way Pearl Harbor affected President Franklin D. Roosevelt and the way the advance of the Communists in Greece and Turkey after World War II affected President Harry S. Truman. From

FDR and Truman, a new policy backing the use of military force and seeking to replace tyranny with democracy quickly emerged. After 9/11, Bush enthusiastically advocated both force and democracy. There's a parallel as well with President William McKinley. Partly as a result of the mysterious explosion that destroyed the battleship *Maine* in Havana harbor, McKinley turned to a revolutionary foreign policy of imperialism, capturing the Philippines and Cuba and trying to implant American political values in each colonial acquisition.

Bush did the same in Afghanistan and Iraq and sought to broaden the reach of democracy to the Middle East and ultimately the entire world. The realist tinge to his foreign policy was gone. Bush had become the world's chief foreign policy idealist. This upset the foreign establishment. "He's a revolutionary and has a revolutionary vision," National Security Adviser Stephen Hadley told me, "and the establishment has a problem with that."

But was he really the source of the radical new direction or merely its mouthpiece? Certainly others have been given a large share of credit, particularly Cheney but also the Defense Department honchos, Rumsfeld and Paul Wolfowitz. The answer is in the evidence. Plenty of evidence points to Bush as the instigator of the bold post-9/11 changes in foreign and national security policy. There is practically none in support of the aides-as-architect thesis, though Wolfowitz's vision of a democratic Middle East sharpened Bush's thinking.

Bush's advisers, speaking on and off the record, tell the same story: the president did it. Of course, his advisers have an interest in praising their boss. They're expected to do that. Yet

they describe Bush's decision-making process quite specifically as one in which he either comes to the table with an idea
in mind (nations that harbor terrorists are as guilty as terrorists themselves) or reaches one or more conclusions during
policy discussions (how to deal with Israel and the Palestinians). It's not that Bush's aides lack influence. In fact, there's
one senior White House aide who deserves credit for swaying
Bush but rarely gets any, Michael Gerson, Bush's handpicked
speechwriter and counselor. Gerson's influence is seen especially in speeches in which the president has taken daring
stands on the Middle East and democracy. The idea of a $15
billion initiative to fight AIDS globally was Gerson's, for
instance. When he suggested it, nearly everyone at the White
House was dubious—except Bush.

HINGE POINT

An event as large and dramatic as 9/11 was bound to alter the
way America deals with the world. Joel Garreau of the *Washington Post* has characterized 9/11 as a historical hinge point.
Such points—he lists 1914, 1929, 1945, 1963, and 1981 as
others in the past century—are "pivots on which our lives
move from one world to another. . . . What changes after a
hinge is our stories of ourselves. Who we are, how we got that
way, where we're headed, and what makes us tick." Bush says
he wasn't personally changed by 9/11, but his presidency was.
His changes in domestic policy included creation of a Department of Homeland Security, enactment of the Patriot Act, and

tightened security at airports. His foreign policy was transformed across the board: on combating terrorism and targeting countries that harbor terrorists, on the appropriate national security strategy and a new plan for the Middle East, on spreading democracy, and on dealing with multilateral organizations and allies, old and new.

Minutes after the attacks, Bush declared that America was at war. And he was determined to win it. That, by itself, established a new policy—an actual war on terrorism—and a new tone. The old policy treated terrorism as a problem for law enforcement. Terrorists were prosecuted after they'd been arrested for committing violent acts. The Bush policy was offensive, not defensive. America would target terrorists on their home turf to disrupt and destroy them before they could mount attacks. Bush first mentioned "war" in a phone call to Cheney less than ten minutes after the second hijacked airliner hit the World Trade Center. "Sounds like we've got a minor war going on here," Bush said. Then, speaking to aides aboard Air Force One, the president escalated his war talk: "We're at war. That's what we're paid for, boys. We're going to take care of this. When we find out who did this, they're not going to like me as president. Somebody's going to pay." From Air Force One, he made another call to Cheney. "We're at war, Dick," he said. "And we're going to find out who did this and we're going to kick their ass." The next morning at the senior staff meeting at the White House, chief of staff Andy Card said, "The president said to act as if we are at war." Later that day, Bush told his National Security Council that the country was at war.

The sharp contrast between the old and new policies on terrorism was described by Cheney in a speech nearly four years after 9/11. The speech didn't attract media attention or stir public discussion:

> Fighting the war on terror has required a shift in our national security policy. For many years prior to 9/11, terror attacks against Americans were treated as isolated incidents, as criminal acts, and answered, if at all, on an ad hoc basis, and rarely in a systematic way. Even after an attack inside our own country—the 1993 bombing at the World Trade Center in New York—there was a tendency to treat terror attacks as criminal acts to be handled primarily through law enforcement.
>
> The main perpetrator of that 1993 attack in New York was tracked down, arrested, convicted, and sent off to serve a 240-year sentence. Yet behind that man was a growing network with operatives inside and outside the United States, waging war against our country. After the World Trade Center attack in 1993 came the murders at the Saudi Arabian National Guard facility in Riyadh in 1995, the simultaneous bombings of our embassies in East Africa—Kenya and Tanzania—in 1998, the bombing of the USS *Cole* in 2000. In 1996, Khalid Sheikh Mohammad, the mastermind of 9/11, first proposed to bin Laden that they use airliners to attack targets in the United States. Later, in 1996 and again in 1998, Osama bin Laden declared war upon the United States. During

the same period, thousands of terrorists were trained at al Qaeda camps throughout Afghanistan.

The President and I understand that America requires an aggressive strategy against these enemies, not merely to prosecute a series of crimes but to fight and win a global campaign against the terror network. There can be no compromise in this mission. Our enemy cannot be deterred, contained, appeased, or negotiated with. It can only be destroyed—and that's the business at hand.

After the success in late 2001 in routing al Qaeda and the Taliban in Afghanistan, the conventional view was that any president would have responded to 9/11 as Bush did. But that's not necessarily the case. Bush's response—"we're at war"—was instinctive. Many of his aides didn't have the same reaction. The next morning, the president met with Republican and Democratic congressional leaders. In his White House memoir *Taking Heat*, Ari Fleischer wrote that one leader balked at Bush's talk of war. "*War* is a very powerful word," the leader said. "This war is so vastly different. Take care in your rhetorical calculations." Fleischer didn't identify the leader. But White House officials told me that it was Tom Daschle, then Senate minority leader.

A week after 9/11, French president Jacques Chirac met with Bush at the White House. Chirac told reporters he stood in solidarity with America, but he, too, recoiled at the president's reference to "a new kind of war." "I don't know whether we should use the word *war*, but what I can say is that now we are faced with a conflict of a completely new nature." Bush instantly saw the high stakes, and subsequent events have confirmed that he reacted correctly.

The president also quickly established what became known as the "Bush doctrine." This was the policy that nations harboring terrorists would be treated as if they were guilty of terrorist acts. "We talked about that the very first night after the attack on 9/11," Cheney told me in an interview. "We'd not only go after the terrorists, we'd go after those who sponsored terror and supported terror" and those who let terrorists operate out of their jurisdiction. "There really wasn't a lot of debate internally," Cheney said. Bush prevailed. At the session with congressional leaders, Bush cited the new policy: "There will be no safe harbor for terrorists," he said. An hour later at a National Security Council meeting, he used more colorful language to characterize the doctrine. "These guys are like rattlesnakes," he said. "They'll go back in their hole. Not only will we strike the hole, we'll strike the rancher." He formally announced the policy a week later in his speech to Congress and the nation.

For Bush, it was important after 9/11 to be clear and unequivocal in his public statements. "I obviously decided to respond forcefully and tried to speak as clearly as I could with the understanding that the more clearly an American president speaks, the easier it is for people to understand what this country is going to do," he told me. "And then make sure when you actually say something, you end up doing it, so that the next time you speak clearly, people understand the words mean something."

As part of the campaign against terrorism, the president turned to a new strategic doctrine, which he called preemption. Since the half-century-old national security strategy of containment was useless against terrorists, the United States would launch a first strike against them before they could attack this country. It wasn't really preemption. Strictly defined, preemption means attacking a foe who is about to attack you. As Yale professor John Lewis Gaddis pointed out, it was a doctrine of preventive war, which means going to war with a group or a nation that might attack you at some future time. Bush, as it happened, had read Gaddis's book *Surprise, Security, and the American Experience*, liked it, and invited Gaddis to the White House for a chat. The president didn't dream up the doctrine, but he kept discussion of it alive. "We'd been talking about it for some time after 9/11," Condoleezza Rice told me. "I would walk in [the Oval Office] in the morning and we would talk about this kind of thing. We would talk about it at the ranch. You know, What does 9/11 mean for the way that we think about how we keep this from happening to us again?"

When Bush adopted the doctrine, it was still amorphous. But the intent of it was clear. "There are certain kinds of threats that are undeterrable," Rice said. "Since terrorists have nothing to lose, they don't have a territory that they defend. They don't have the attributes of a state, which is what you use to deter people. You had to go to a doctrine that says we will get them before they get us."

The doctrine took shape once Bush decided to announce it in a graduation address in June 2002 at West Point. The speechmaking process, led by Bush and Gerson, "makes you kind of focus on it and crystallize it," Rice said. Bush spent a month and a half honing the remarks. Some speeches excite the press and generate extravagant coverage. Important as it was, the West Point speech didn't. The problem was that few reporters understood the message or, as a Bush aide said, "broke the code." Bush, however, was explicit. "New threats require new thinking," he said. "I will not stand by as peril grows closer and closer. . . . If we wait for [terrorist] threats to fully materialize, we will have waited too long." America, he said, will take "preemptive action when necessary." Indeed, America would do exactly that in Iraq.

FLIPPING THE CONVENTIONAL WISDOM ON ITS HEAD

Up to the moment Bush became president, his predecessor, Bill Clinton, was desperately pressing for an Israeli-Palestinian peace accord. He failed, mostly because of Yasser Arafat's intransigence. Bush took a different tack. And he devised the strategy, not his aides. Whatever the conventional wisdom was, Bush "would flip it on its head," according to Hadley. "Some people say terror has to end first and then you can talk about building democratic institutions," Hadley said. "He would say, Of course we have to fight terror, but at the end of the day the way to defeat terror over the long term is build democratic institutions."

Regarding Arafat, the popular notion was that only through working with him was peace possible. Bush decided that the opposite was true: only by shoving Arafat aside was peace possible. "The foreign policy community was appalled by this statement," Hadley told me.

The president had a third insight as well: Israelis will feel comfortable living next to a Palestinian state only if it's democratic. "If you establish a state of that character, that's the only kind of state that Israel will be willing to make the kind of hard decisions that we know Israel will have to make" as part of a final peace settlement, Hadley said.

Taken together, Bush's insights constitute a strategic view of the Israeli-Palestinian struggle that departs radically from the view of the prior half-century. Europeans, the Arab states, and most Middle East experts criticized Bush harshly. But by the start of his second term, his view had become the new consensus.

The president's belief in the power of democracy reached far beyond the small chunk of the Middle East inhabited by Israelis and Palestinians. Over five years—one as a candidate, four as president—Bush gradually moved toward proclaiming an aggressive worldwide crusade for democracy. Of course he would never use the word *crusade* for fear of angering Muslims, but that's what his pro-democracy drive is. (Bush had been stung by criticism when he uttered the word *crusade* once in 2002 and didn't use it again.) This effort puts him in the camp with one former president in particular, Woodrow Wilson, who pleaded with his British and French allies in World War I to abandon imperialism and let democracy flower in their colonies. They refused. This time, the president chose to lean directly on the leaders of insufficiently democratic countries, including friendly autocrats such as Hosni Mubarak of Egypt and Vladimir Putin of Russia. The push for democracy allowed Bush to seize the moral high ground in foreign policy.

Well before 9/11, Bush voiced his skepticism about multilateral organizations and treaties. This was a dramatic switch from the Clinton years, when acting multilaterally, never unilaterally, was prescribed. Bush abruptly pulled out of the Kyoto global warming treaty, to the consternation of Europeans and environmentalists. He withdrew from the Anti-Ballistic Missile Treaty with Russia, upsetting liberals and a handful of Cold War intellectuals. The critics claimed an arms race would follow. Bush said it wouldn't. Bush turned out to be right. When the president ordered the invasion of Iraq without the explicit approval of the United Nations Security Council, he was accused of being a dangerous unilateralist. Bush defended unilateralism in theory but didn't practice it. In confronting North Korea and its nuclear weapons program, Bush rejected a solo U.S. role and insisted on six-party talks that brought in China, Japan, and South Korea. In Iraq, Bush, at one time or another, attracted thirty to thirty-five countries to his side. Of these, Britain was the most important. It not only sent the most troops, it also lent the cachet of a major power to Bush's Iraq policy and bolstered his legitimacy as a war president.

But had Bush's radical new policy strengthened America's position in the world? To answer that, consider the state of play when Bush took office in January 2001. Afghanistan was a sanctuary for terrorists. Pakistan was the chief proliferator of nuclear-weapons expertise and material and was evolving into a terrorist state. The Saudis were funding al Qaeda. A second Palestinian intifada had led to bloody attacks on Israel. Iraq was a menace. Libya had an aggressive program to build weapons of mass destruction. The terrorist threat to America was building. And terrorism was growing in southeast Asia.

Now Afghanistan and Iraq are pro-American democracies. Both Pakistan and its rival, India, are allies of the United States. Saudi Arabia is of less help to al Qaeda, which has been weakened. Libya has disarmed. Israel and the Palestinians are closer to a peace settlement than at any time in decades. Since the Iraqi election on January 30, 2005, popular pressure for democracy has broken out in the Middle East. Lebanese, both Muslims and Christians, staged the Cedar Revolution, which, along with pressure from the United States and France, forced Syria to withdraw its troops from Lebanon. Free elections followed in Lebanon and democratic stirrings were detected in Syria. And in Egypt, President Hosni Mubarak, who normally insisted on running for reelection unopposed, agreed to allow an opponent on the ballot in late 2005. And that once-hostile region, according to Arab scholar Fouad Ajami, is now "Bush country." So the answer is yes, America's strategic position has indeed been fortified.

At the beginning of Bush's second term, Silvio Berlusconi, the Italian prime minister, told an American visitor that he was "Bush's best friend in Europe, better than Tony Blair." It wasn't so. Blair proved his loyalty to Bush over and over. The G8 summit of industrial democracies met in Canada the day after the president had ostracized Yasser Arafat. Of the G8 leaders, Blair alone defended Bush's decision. At great political risk, Blair has been a steadfast ally in Iraq. And like former prime minister Margaret Thatcher, he has often made plain his affection for America. In a speech to Congress in 2003, he said America has a central role in Iraq—and the larger struggle against terrorism—"because destiny put you in this place in history, in this moment in time, and the task is yours to do." He added that Americans must never apologize for their values or be afraid to "tell the world why you are proud of America." Americans stand for the "Star-Spangled Banner" because of that pride, he indicated, "not because some state official told them to."

Nearly every Tuesday, Bush and Blair talk by teleconference. Sir Martin Gilbert, the great British historian, has written that "some comparisons are already clear" between the wartime alliance of Bush and Blair and the partnership of FDR and Winston Churchill in World War II. Bush once said at a meeting with Blair, "I am a lucky person, a lucky president, to be holding office at the same time this man holds the prime ministership." Blair was just as lucky to hold office while Bush was president.

Chapter 4

Reversal: Reinventing America's Role in the Middle East

PRESIDENT CLINTON WAS ANGRY. It was his last day in office, January 20, 2001, and he was still furious at Palestinian leader Yasser Arafat. Arafat had played him for a fool in negotiations over a peace settlement between the Palestinians and Israel. And Clinton knew it. A few days earlier, in one of their last conversations, Arafat had thanked Clinton for all he'd done to achieve a Middle East accord. He praised Clinton as a great man. Clinton was having none of it. "Mr. Chairman," Clinton said, using Arafat's title as head of the Palestinian Authority, "I am not a great man. I am a failure, and you have made me one." Arafat's refusal to come to terms with Israel, Clinton said, would lead to the election of Ariel Sharon, the tough ex-general, as Israeli prime misister. And Arafat would "reap a whirlwind."

Now Clinton was giving President-elect George W. Bush an earful. It was the traditional one-on-one meeting over tea between the old and new presidents just before their limousine ride to the Capitol for the inauguration ceremony. When

Jimmy Carter and Ronald Reagan met in 1981, Carter lectured the new president from note cards on a list of subjects. Afterward, Reagan asked for the note cards. The Clinton-Bush meeting was short, only a few minutes, and Clinton concentrated on a single subject—Arafat. He didn't need note cards.

The previous summer Clinton had hosted a summit between Arafat and Israeli president Ehud Barak at Camp David. Barak had made extraordinary concessions, offering to give up the Arab quarter of Jerusalem and all but a small fraction of the West Bank. Arafat had balked. Worse, he had either ordered a new round of deadly violence against Israelis or acquiesced in the renewal of attacks. Still, Clinton had not been ready to give up. He had drafted his own set of unofficial "ideas" for a settlement. They weren't American policy, but they could be if Arafat agreed to them. They were even more generous in their concessions to the Palestinians than those offered at Camp David. Arafat balked again. So Clinton invited him to the White House for a face-to-face showdown on January 2. Arafat argued, obfuscated, and quibbled. "His body language said no, but the deal was so good I couldn't believe anyone would be foolish enough to let it go," Clinton later wrote in his memoir *My Life.* Arafat's aides and the ambassadors to America from Egypt and Saudia Arabia prodded him to say yes. But he never gave Clinton an answer. In effect, that meant no.

Clinton's sense of betrayal and his doubts about Arafat's willingness to accept peace with Israel on any terms made a strong impression on Bush. When he became president, Bush was not entirely a dilettante on the subject of Israel and the Middle East. But he wasn't well versed either. His major foreign policy speech of the 2000 presidential campaign had dismissed the Middle East in a single lonely sentence. "An American president," Bush had said, "should defend America's interests in the Persian Gulf and advance peace in the Middle East, based upon a secure Israel." For Bush, Clinton was an expert whose advice counted. And what he said hardly inclined Bush to embrace the tangled issue as president. Peace in the Middle East seemed distant, perhaps unattainable. Thus, true to predictions, including Clinton's, Bush put the issue on the back burner. China, Russia, and an overstuffed domestic agenda loomed larger in Bush's mind than Israelis and Palestinians. He met with Ariel Sharon, who had indeed been elected Israeli prime minister in reaction to Palestinian terrorist bombings. But he pointedly passed up a chance to greet Arafat at the United Nations and did nothing to revive the peace process.

Then came 9/11. The attacks on the World Trade Center and the Pentagon put the United States in the same vulnerable position as Israel. Both were targets of Muslim terrorists. Shortly after 9/11, Bush declared those who harbor terrorists as culpable as terrorists themselves. This implicated Arafat, who gave terrorist organizations free rein in Palestinian territory. And as terrorist attacks continued in Israel, Arafat didn't lift a finger to halt them. In January 2002, a ship with fifty tons of rockets, mortar, grenades, and explosives from Iran, the *Karine A*, was apprehended by Israeli naval commandos as it headed to a rendezvous with Palestinian terrorists. Arafat denied any knowledge of the shipment, sending Bush a note to that effect. The president soon learned from intelligence sources that Arafat was lying.

Meanwhile, Arab leaders such as Crown Prince Abdullah of Saudi Arabia had been urging the Bush administration for months to revive the peace process. In the spring, Bush relented. And the consequences of his decision were as far-reaching as they were unexpected. The policy followed by every American administration since Israel was formally recognized in 1948 came tumbling down. In a string of meetings in the Situation Room in the basement of the White House during the spring of 2002, a new policy was hammered out at Bush's instigation. It amounted to a revolution in Middle East diplomacy.

Nixon, Ford, Carter, Reagan, Bush's father, and Clinton were too conventional in their thinking to conceive a radical new policy, much less pull one off. Bush was not. He was the architect of the new policy. And by the outset of Bush's second term, peace between the Israelis and the Palestinians was no longer a distant hope. The president's approach to the Middle East had quickly become the "new consensus" and was "beginning to have some effects," National Security Adviser Stephen Hadley told me.

Bush announced the policy shift in the Rose Garden on June 24, 2002, with his national security advisers at his side. Arafat would be banished, though he was not mentioned by name in Bush's speech. Neither Bush nor any American official would meet with him. He was part of the problem, not the solution. "Peace requires a new and different Palestinian leadership, so that a Palestinian state can be born," Bush said. He had never accepted the idea that there was no alternative to Arafat. Former press secretary Ari Fleischer tells in *Taking Heat*, his White House memoir, of a dramatic encounter between Bush and a Middle East leader several weeks before the Rose Garden speech. "What do you mean, there's no alternative to Arafat?" the president said as he leaned forward in his chair and pointed his finger. "I have more faith in the Arab people than you do. Surely there's a Palestinian leader better than Yasser Arafat. Of course there is."

The president broke more new ground by endorsing a two-state scheme: the division of Palestine between Israel and independent, democratic Palestine and the two living side by side in peace. This had been implicit in Clinton's policy, but Bush was the first president to espouse it publicly. Full diplomatic recognition would come, he said, "when the Palestinian people have new leaders, new institutions, and new security arrangements with their neighbors." It would require full-blown democracy and an end to terrorism, the president declared. "Today, Palestinian authorities are encouraging, not opposing, terrorism," he said, stating the obvious.

Bush paid less attention to Israel. He said fresh "settlement activity" in Palestinian areas and Israel's military occupation of the West Bank and Gaza must cease. But there was an important change in the American-Israeli relationship that Bush did not make public. He hinted at it when he insisted Israelis have "a right to security." Two months earlier he had said Sharon should withdraw Israeli troops and tanks that had charged into Palestinian cities to capture terrorists, but he put no pressure on Sharon to implement a withdrawal. Indeed, when dispatching Secretary of State Colin Powell to the Middle East, Bush criticized Arafat and endorsed "Israel's right to defend itself from terror." The unannounced change was to allow Israel to defend itself aggressively without complaint or second-guessing from Washington. Bush might question Sharon about the exact route of the security fence under construction between Israel and the West Bank. But after initially criticizing the fence, Bush would treat it as a legitimate part of Israel's defense. On a more sensitive issue, Bush would allow Israeli forces to assassinate the leaders of terrorist groups that were murdering Israelis.

There was still another change in American policy that went unstated but was implicit in Bush's announcement. This involved reciprocity. For decades, nothing tangible had been required of the Palestinians. Arafat had repeatedly agreed to clamp down on terrorists, but that was a promise he had never been forced to keep. While Israel frequently agreed to risky steps in peace negotiations, the Palestinians took none. Strange as it seems, Israeli concessions were matched by American concessions: the United States would step in with security guarantees. So when Israel gave up the Sinai Peninsula, which it had seized in the 1967 Six-Day War, it got warplanes from the United States in return. And as part of the 1993 Oslo Agreement between Israel and the Palestinians, the United States again responded with weapons and also loan guarantees.

Bush's speech signaled the termination of that one-sided arrangement. This time much was demanded of the Palestinians, everything from new leaders to a new form of government. For Bush, there would be no turning back to the easy-going days in which the Palestinians were always to be accommodated, never to be challenged. The old policy, a Bush aide said, was simply an international version of "the soft bigotry of low expectations."

The whole of Bush's stunning policy reversal on the Middle East was greater than the sum of its parts. It was even more sweeping than it looked. Imposing serious requirements on the Palestinians meant that the practice of leaning solely on Israel was dead. For decades, "reengagement" in the peace process and "accelerating" the peace process were euphemisms for pressuring the Israelis for new concessions. No more. Just as significant, Bush applied a performance-based yardstick for progress toward a peace settlement. In the past, progress toward peace had been time-based, and Palestinian shortcomings were routinely ignored to keep up with the timetable. Bush dumped that practice.

A year later the president further obligated the Palestinians to perform—to create democratic institutions and quash terrorism—when he approved the "road map" to Middle East peace devised by the "quartet" of Britain, Russia, the European Union, and the United States. Its three steps were based purely on performance. And the hoary precept of land for peace—in which Israel was called upon to give up land in Gaza and the West Bank in exchange for peaceful behavior by the Palestinians—was also relegated to the dustbin. The trouble with that precept had been that the Palestinians hadn't delivered peace. Bush installed the idea of peace for peace.

Two democratic states would guarantee peace to each other, the objections of Israelis and conservative American Jews to a separate Palestinian state having long since faded.

A DIFFERENT TACK

The president's unanticipated handling of the Middle East had a preface. In late November and early December 1998, Bush and three other Republican governors—Mike Leavitt of Utah, Marc Racicot of Montana, and Paul Cellucci of Massachusetts—toured Israel along with their wives. Bush, fresh from his landslide reelection as governor of Texas, had all but made up his mind to run for president in 2000. He was the star of the trip, which lasted a week and allowed the governors to meet the whole spectrum of Israeli political figures. They smoked cigars at the home of Benjamin Netanyahu, then Israeli prime minister and leader of the conservative Likud Party. They sat down with Barak and Shimon Peres, both Labor Party stalwarts. They traveled the Via Dolorosa and read Scripture at the Church of the Holy Sepulchre. At the church, "everyone had tears in their eyes," said Matt Brooks, executive director of the Republican Jewish Coalition and organizer of the trip.

Brooks had sought for months to line up a meeting with Arafat. "We thought they should get a balanced view," he told me. "We didn't want to stack the deck." But Arafat wouldn't agree to a meeting. Then, to Bush's surprise, the Palestinian Authority announced that Bush had turned down an invitation to meet with Arafat. Bush chose not to stage a public spat with the Palestinians, and he let the matter drop. "It was an enlightening introduction for him to the Palestinians and Arafat," Brooks said.

The highlight of the trip was a helicopter ride over Israel with Ariel Sharon as the guide. Sharon was foreign minister at the time and widely viewed as a man in the twilight of his career. U.S. State Department officials accompanying the governors were leery of the helicopter jaunt. They warned against flying over territory Israel had captured in the 1967 war, fearing it would inflame Palestinian sensitivities. Bush said he didn't "give a shit what the State Department said." The helicopter flew over the disputed area. The purpose of the trip, however, was to show Israel's vulnerability by flying over its narrowest point, nine miles wide. "We've got drive-ways longer than that in Texas," Bush quipped. Bush also met the pilots from the squadron that had bombed the Iraqi nuclear facility at Osirak in 1981. That raid had piqued Bush's interest. He thanked the pilots for successfully executing the mission—a model for a strategic and effective "preemptive" strike.

But when Bush began campaigning for president in 1999, he gave little indication of how he would deal with Israel. Howard Kohr, the executive director of the American Israel Public Affairs Committee, better known as the pro-Israel lobby, told me that he didn't have the foggiest idea. Bush had gotten along well with Sharon on his trip to Israel, and he also recruited defense intellectual Paul Wolfowitz, a strong supporter of Israel, as a senior campaign adviser on foreign affairs.

But Bush's family connections raised questions. His father's experience with Israel had been contentious and unpleasant, especially his dealings with Yitzhak Shamir, the unyielding prime minister. (In fact, the elder Bush had caused his son to arrive several days late for his 1998 visit to Israel when he arranged for his son to fly to Egypt beforehand and meet with President Hosni Mubarak, with whom Bush senior was more friendly.) "Given [Bush's] genetic endowment—his father— you'd have thought he'd be bad on Israel," a senior Bush adviser told me. His father's top advisers bolstered that impression. His secretary of state, James A. Baker III, was regarded as hostile to Israel and chummy with Israel's Arab adversaries. His national security adviser, Brent Scowcroft, was correctly seen as a sharp and undeviating critic of Israel.

Once George W. Bush entered the White House, he appointed few allies of Israel to his national security team or to the State Department. His own national security adviser, Condoleezza Rice, was a protégé of Scowcroft's. Yet when Bush sat in National Security Council (NSC) meetings in 2002 to craft a policy on the Middle East, almost all his insights were favorable to Israel. The meetings brought together the president, Vice President Dick Cheney, Powell, Defense Secretary Donald Rumsfeld, Rice, and George Tenet, the director of the Central Intelligence Agency. Rumsfeld's presence was important. The defense secretary is not automatically a participant in foreign policy discussions at the White House. But when the NSC is the venue for the deliberations, the defense secretary takes part as a full NSC member.

Rumsfeld was sympathetic to Israel and so were his top aides, including Deputy Defense Secretary Wolfowitz.

Michael Gerson, Bush's chief speechwriter, was among the administration staffers who sat along the wall at the meetings, not participating but listening intently. He was impressed by the high tone, the thoroughness, and the complete lack of animosity among the principals, even when they disagreed. "It was just the way you hoped government would be," he told me.

Cheney turned out to be as pro-Israel and tough on Arafat and the Palestinians as Bush and Rumsfeld were. He had no confidence in the proposals announced sporadically to reduce tensions over security between the Israelis and the Palestinians. When the ship *Karine A*, loaded with arms for Palestinian terrorists, was apprehended, Cheney took a hard line. It wasn't a minor Palestinian transgression, he said. It was further evidence of Arafat's lack of interest in making peace. Arafat must have known about the shipment. Once more, Powell and the State Department took a softer line. Their recommendation was to make sure the Palestinians would never try to import a large cache of arms again. For Bush, though, the *Karine A* episode was the last straw. After that, he was prepared to cast Arafat aside.

The State Department was not as ready to abandon the Palestinian leader. When Vice President Cheney went to the Middle East in 2002, he didn't plan to see Arafat. The trip was intended to give the vice president an opportunity to talk to Middle East leaders about freeing Iraq and deposing Saddam

Hussein. The 9/11 attacks had altered how Bush and his foreign policy team viewed Iraq. Stephen Hadley told me, "9/11 changed our views about the acceptability of risks." And Saddam posed many. His hatred of America, his connections with terrorists, his suspected (but later disproved) access to weapons of mass destruction, his history of invading neighboring countries and massacring his own people—all made him a threat to the United States. Cheney's message was not that Bush had decided on war with Iraq, only that war had become a distinct possibility unless Saddam reformed. In the meantime, the State Department wanted Cheney to drop by Arafat's headquarters. The question of whether he would or not hung over the vice president's trip.

Cheney was willing to see Arafat on one condition: the Palestinian would have to sign an interim security agreement arranged by a Powell aide, General Anthony Zinni. The pact looked like a done deal. Arafat had already agreed to it. His practice was normally to sign agreements, then violate them. For once, he took a different tack. He declined to sign, stiffing Cheney in the process.

After Colin Powell had met with Arafat earlier that year, he said he was probably the last American official who would speak to the Palestinian leader. And he was.

Bush told me that his decision to dump Arafat had a positive effect. "I happen to think my decision on Arafat caused the world to think differently about the problem and recognize that in order for there to be two states, there has to be a democracy run by leaders who are not corrupt and who care about the people [and] where the people make the decisions," the president said. "It wasn't the most popular statement I've ever made in terms of world opinion, which is fine." Now, Bush said, "if you were to ask people that might have been critical initially, they'd say, 'Well, maybe he was right.'"

PROBLEM SOLVER

If any doubts lingered, after 9/11 and the war in Afghanistan, about Bush's ability to take charge of foreign affairs, they were dispelled as he deftly moved his administration toward a new policy on Israel and the Palestinians. "One of the things people can't see is how strategically incisive the president can be," Rice told me. "He can see out there a different direction, and then once he's established that we have to have a different direction and really has come to the essence of what it ought to be," his clarity helps his staff carry out the new policy. In other words, Bush decides, his aides follow and work out the details. "The Middle East is a perfect example of this," Rice said.

With speechwriter Gerson in the Situation Room, Bush's thoughts, conclusions, and rhetorical questions often cropped up later in his speeches. His first question in the discussions sometimes did. Bush asked, "Who has ever cared about the Palestinian people?" Everyone knew the answer. No one had cared—not Israel, not Arab countries, not Palestinian leaders, not Muslim jihadists, not anyone. Bush's response to that question came in his June 24, 2002, speech. Democracy, new leaders, and an end to terrorism were paramount. But there was more. "The Palestinian people live in economic stagnation, made worse by official corruption," he said. "A Palestinian state will require a vibrant economy, where honest enterprise is encouraged by an honest government." America and international organizations would reform Palestinian finances. "And the United States, along with our partners in the developed world, will increase our humanitarian assistance to relieve Palestinian suffering," he said. "The world is prepared to help."

Bush came to two conclusions about Israel during the policy discussions. One, Israelis truly desire peace but would never accept a final settlement with a terrorist state that had the untrustworthy Arafat as its leader. Israel would wait as long as necessary for an acceptable leader, not tied to terrorists, to emerge. The president's thinking was no doubt shaped by the 1998 trip to Israel, all the more so by his later conversations with Sharon. Two, Bush decided that hectoring Sharon whenever he did something that upset American diplomats was counterproductive. Bush's main job was to gain Sharon's trust. If he achieved that, if Sharon was convinced Bush would stand with him unflinchingly, then Sharon would feel more comfortable in making concessions as part of a peace deal. To this end, Bush halted the State Department's practice of publicly condemning Israel whenever it killed a Palestinian terrorist leader.

With his aversion to "small-ball," it was natural for the president to bring up the basic question of the root causes of Middle East turmoil. Why not deal with the real source of the problem, instead of bothering with marginal issues? "The way the Middle East and the Israeli-Palestinian issue was thought of for years and years and years, it was all about borders," Rice told me. "It was all about what were going to be the borders to the Palestinian state." It was as if drawing the right borders would produce peace. Bush changed the subject. He focused on the Palestinian leadership and whether it wanted peaceful coexistence with Israel. After the horrific Passover bombing of a Jewish seder in Israel that spring, Bush and Rice had intense private discussions about Arafat and his cohorts. The president's sense, Rice said, was "that until you got Palestinian leadership that was really prepared to put aside violence and was prepared to lead the people someplace other than where they were going, it was not going to be possible to get peace."

Bush's preference for making big decisions came into play. He hates to manage a problem or a dispute or a broken relationship. In almost every issue discussion at the White House, Bush asks, "What's the solution?" He views himself primarily as a problem solver. And the solution in the Middle East was clear to him: Arafat had to go. Bush had insinuated as much in a statement on the day of the Passover bombing. Arafat had agreed to stop terror attacks, the president said, but "he's not done so. . . . He's missed his opportunities and thereby betrayed the hopes of the people he's supposed to lead." On June 24, Bush was unequivocal. "Peace requires a new and different Palestinian leadership, so that a Palestinian state can be born," he said.

Bush didn't stop there. It wasn't enough to make Arafat persona non grata. The larger problem was that Arafat was the leader of a corrupt, terrorist state. It was the institution— the Arafat model—that needed to be uprooted as well. And the president's obligation was to spell out the parameters of power for the person who would follow Arafat. Bush did precisely that. "True reform will require entirely new political and economic institutions, based on democracy, market economics, and action against terrorism," he said. A constitution that mandated a separation of powers and an elected parliament was required. The old ways had to be swept out totally.

But what if he hadn't gone so far in his demands? What if he had failed to make Arafat a pariah and denounce his brand of government? The consequences would have been disastrous. When Arafat died in November 2004, his successor, Mahmoud Abbas, might well have modeled himself after Arafat. The world might have accepted that. But because Bush made it clear that the Arafat model would never lead to a Palestinian state, the tacit assumption was that Arafat's successor would be chosen through a democratic election, conducted fairly and honestly. He was. The turnout was huge, and Abbas won the vote overwhelmingly. As Palestinian president, he has renounced terrorism. He has begun doing what Arafat never did, arrest Palestinian terrorists. And he is pursuing a peace deal with Israel.

Bush achieved a Middle East breakthrough that had eluded his predecessors. His insights were the basis for a policy reversal that has transformed the prospects for peace. But he has received no praise for this outside of Israel. He has instead received persistent criticism. But imagine if these same insights—institutions matter most, geopolitical problems should be solved instead of managed—had been authored by a respected strategist in international affairs such as former secretary of state Henry Kissinger. The world would be in awe of his conceptual abilities.

The day after his June 24 speech, the president flew to Canada for the annual summit of the world's eight industrial democracies. He was not given a hero's welcome. With the lone exception of British prime minister Tony Blair, the G8 leaders "went kind of crazy about the idea the president had said Arafat had to go," Rice told me. French president Jacques Chirac stated the conventional wisdom: peace in the Middle East depended on dealing with Arafat. But Bush held firm. Two years later, in fact, he took a further step, rejecting the Palestinians' key demand to allow the return to Israel of descendants of those who owned land there prior to Israeli independence in 1948. These refugees should settle in a new Palestinian state, not Israel, Bush said. The president also said that "already existing major Israeli population centers" should remain as part of Israel. Bush again drew criticism, but far less than before. The stigma he had pasted on Arafat was taking hold.

There's a historical what-if in the story of Bush's policy flip. What if nineteen Islamic extremists had not flown commercial airliners into the World Trade Center and the Pentagon on September 11, 2001? Bush had intended to make a dramatic announcement in a speech to the United Nations in mid-September. He was going to throw his support to a two-state solution, a sovereign Palestinian state at peace with neighboring Israel. That would have constituted a partial change in policy, and Bush would have been the first American president to endorse that option publicly. But the Bush announcement would not have included insistence on Arafat's ouster or a demand for sweeping democratic reform of the Palestinian government. Arafat would have been spared the president's public wrath. September 11 intervened, the speech was canceled, and Bush was given more time to deliberate on the Middle East. It was time well spent.

Chapter 5

Unflinching: Bringing
Democracy to Iraq

IT SNOWED LIGHTLY IN WASHINGTON on Sunday, January 30, 2005. And from outward appearances there wasn't
much going on at the White House—no celebration anyway,
and no gloating either. President Bush skipped church. He
checked the news on TV in the morning and worked on a
statement to the press. At exactly 1 P.M., he stood in the foyer
of the White House and read the statement to a small pool
of reporters and television cameras. He praised the citizens of
Iraq for voting earlier that day "in great numbers and under
great risk" and showing "their commitment to democracy."
They had "taken rightful control of their country's destiny," the
president said. It was "a great and historic achievement."
Bush's delivery, a pool reporter wrote, was "firm and unre-
markable." The statement took five minutes, after which Bush
turned and left. He took no questions. It was his only public
appearance of the day.

Out of public view, the White House was busy. Bush
talked once to his new secretary of state, Condoleezza Rice,

and twice to Stephen Hadley, who had succeeded Rice as national security adviser. He telephoned Egyptian president Hosni Mubarak, King Abdullah of Jordan, and Saudi Arabia's Crown Prince Abdullah, the Middle East leaders whose countries might be aroused if Iraqi democracy proved to be contagious.

Bush and his aides shared a feeling of satisfaction and a sense that Iraq had passed a turning point. "Until that day, you didn't know how it would turn out in Iraq," press secretary Scott McClellan told me. The election meant that the forces of democracy would almost surely prevail. But the president had learned, painfully, not to overplay his hand on Iraq. After the three-week war that ousted Saddam Hussein, Bush had flown in May 2003 to the deck of the USS *Lincoln*, an aircraft carrier in the Pacific, and declared the end of major combat. Behind him was a large banner saying, "MISSION ACCOMPLISHED." The Bush theatrics became an embarrassment when the postwar insurrection by Saddam loyalists and Islamic extremists intensified over the summer. In fact, Bush hadn't claimed victory. It had only seemed as if he had because of the banner. This time, his public response was solemn. "There's more distance to travel on the road to democracy," he said.

Yet for Bush, January 30 was Vindication Day. Once al Qaeda and the Taliban had been subdued in Afghanistan, Iraq was the next target. The president and his advisers believed that confrontation with Saddam Hussein was inevitable. The official U.S. policy on Iraq, adopted by President Clinton in 1998 and ratified by Bush, was regime change—peacefully if possible, militarily if not. That policy reflected the fact that Saddam was a menace to the Middle East, to Europe, to the United States. His missiles could already reach Western Europe, and his scientists were working frantically to extend their range. Saddam had invaded two of his neighbors, Iran and Kuwait, and seemed likely to invade again. He had used weapons of mass destruction (WMD) on his own people and, it seemed, could use them on others. Saddam's ties to terrorists were alarming as well. He harbored foreign terrorists, let terrorist gangs train in Iraq, and rewarded the parents of Palestinian suicide bombers with checks for $25,000. For Saddam, terrorists could be the delivery vehicle for his WMD, even slipping into the United States to wreak violent havoc. And he was a megalomaniac, a cold-blooded killer with grandiose ideas of becoming the master of the entire Arab world and a willingness to challenge the United States. Sooner or later, he would have to be dealt with.

But President Bush had been urged not to invade. That advice came not only from liberals and isolationists but also from a sprinkling of Republicans, the media, Europeans, Chinese, and other foreigners. His father's national security adviser, Brent Scowcroft, had written that military intervention in Iraq would "divert us for some indefinite period from our war on terrorism" and would touch off "an explosion of outrage against us" in the Middle East. James A. Baker III, his father's secretary of state, had also expressed misgivings. And his own secretary of state at the time, Colin Powell, had qualms. A small army of retired generals feared for the worst. Bush bought none of the arguments about containing, but not conquering, Iraq.

There was also a political calculation. Swift success in Afghanistan had driven up Bush's popularity. War in Iraq would put that at risk. His reelection in 2004 might be jeopardized. But the quick victory in the war seemed to justify the risk. Then came the ugly postwar situation. For Bush, it was a period of unexpected agony. The invasion of Iraq had led to looting, sabotage of oil pipelines and electricity, a bloody uprising marked by car bombs, the killing of more than a thousand American soldiers, the Abu Ghraib prison scandal, and the humiliating failure to find weapons of mass destruction.

But it was not the unrelenting violence and terrorism in Iraq or the embarrassments that caused the greatest worry for the president. It was the Iraqi election scheduled for January 30, 2005. As he was "getting ready to roll in the second term," Bush told me, "there was a lot of anxiety in the media and elsewhere about Iraq. There was intense focus about whether or not this election process would work." He fretted over Christmas and through the inauguration over this. He pumped Rice with questions, he recalled. "You know, 'Do you think they're going to vote? What do you think?' Of course, we [were] all hoping. We all believe[d] it. And sure enough, they showed up by the millions."

Indeed they did show up.

On January 30, the Iraqis embraced democracy and elected their own government. Three months later, the Senate, including John Kerry and vociferous Iraq critics like Teddy Kennedy and Robert Byrd, voted 100–0 to continue the American effort in Iraq.

Bush had received vindication both abroad and at home.

When I asked whether he felt vindicated, however, the president responded that he couldn't concern himself with such thoughts. "You can't worry about being vindicated," he told me, "because the truth of the matter is when you do big things, it's going to take a while for history to really understand."

Success in at least laying the foundation for representative government in Iraq had many authors—General Tommy Franks and the U.S. military, American envoy L. Paul Bremer, Shiite Ayatollah Ali al-Sistani, a swarm of pro-freedom Iraqis—but one in particular stands out. That's Bush. Without his unflinching commitment to the Iraq mission and the strategy for accomplishing it, there would be no free and democratic Iraq.

Bush was steadfast at the most important decision points in postwar Iraq, despite conflicting advice. He refused to consider installing an unelected strongman to bring instant stability to Iraq. On this, he rejected the policy guidance of the State Department. He turned down without a second thought a French recommendation to transfer management of postwar Iraq to the United Nations, even though many prominent Democrats and members of the American foreign policy establishment viewed the proposal sympathetically. He backed Bremer at critical moments, dismissing the criticism of him by conservatives in Washington. He decided, in spite of pressure from congressional Republicans, to finance Iraqi reconstruction by U.S. grants, not loans. And he insisted on keeping the schedules for the handover of sovereignty to the Iraqis and for the national election.

Bush didn't make these decisions out of the blue. His

day-to-day engagement in the war on terrorism after 9/11 is well known. The same hands-on style continued during the war in Iraq and through the postwar period. Bush and his war cabinet—Rice, Powell, Vice President Cheney, Defense Secretary Donald Rumsfeld, CIA Director George Tenet, General Richard Myers—held a weekly teleconference with Bremer and the top generals in Iraq. Bush liked crisp sessions without whining or complaints. Once he had to interrupt a discussion of troop rotation to say, "Stop the hand wringing!" The other problem was the teleconference system itself. It occasionally froze. Andy Card, the White House chief of staff, made sure that Bremer had easy phone access to the president. When Rice took over as Iraq coordinator from Rumsfeld several months after the war, she talked several times daily to Bremer and kept the president informed.

Bremer was often called back to Washington either to meet directly with Bush or to testify on Capitol Hill. But Bush didn't rely entirely on Bremer. In late September 2003, he and a dozen officials, mostly civilians, who'd served in Iraq gathered in the Roosevelt Room. It was a relaxed meeting, with the group sitting around a large table, Bush in the middle and Rice and Card on each side. He asked the officials to describe an experience they'd had in Iraq, then pumped them with questions. Dan Senor, Bremer's spokesman and adviser, talked about the fledgling Iraqi media. He described them as diverse and raucous and immature but learning the ways of an independent press corps. Ryan Crocker, later named ambassador to Pakistan, told stories about the blossoming political process. Joanne Dickow, a Pentagon official whose ancestors were Chaldean Christians in Iraq, explained how proud she was to have the opportunity to help Iraqis. Listening to her, Bush got choked up.

THE MOVE TOWARD DEMOCRACY

The idea of a strongman in charge of Iraq—who'd be neither an absolute dictator nor a democratic leader forced to adhere to public opinion—was discussed well before the war in Iraq. It had little appeal to the president, but he allowed a debate to go on for months without expressing an opinion. It was no surprise that the State Department pushed the idea. American diplomats often find nondemocratic leaders easier to deal with and indeed have close relationships with many of them, especially in the Middle East.

The question, Rice told me, was "if we do take down Saddam Hussein's government, what is America's responsibility to what kind of Iraq? Were you just talking about introducing a kind of stable government, or did it have to be a democratic government? We had pretty extensive discussions." Cheney, for one, was firmly opposed to a strongman. Though installing such a leader "would have been easy to do," the vice president told me, Cheney felt that State Department experts pushing that approach had "a limited view of the capacity of a lot of people out there for self-government." Bush likewise didn't share the experts' view. When he finally waded in, he was adamant about a democratic Iraq. Hence, no strongman.

Bush wasn't inclined to like anything French either. The

French had viciously undermined him at the UN, not merely opposing a resolution authorizing the removal of Saddam Hussein but actively campaigning against it. Bush felt this was a hostile act. He loathed French president Jacques Chirac every bit as much as he disliked UN Secretary-General Kofi Annan. So Chirac's proposal to give the UN the job of creating a new Iraqi government and rebuilding the country's infrastructure was destined to go nowhere. One reason was Annan's broken promise about keeping a UN presence in Iraq after its Baghdad headquarters was bombed in August 2003, killing the top UN official, Sérgio de Mello, and seventeen others. Annan assured Bremer that the UN mission would stay. The next day, he announced its pullout. Later, Annan claimed that the invasion of Iraq had been illegal.

In an interview I conducted for this book, one of the president's closest advisers, who reliably reflects the president's thinking on foreign policy, furiously attacked the UN performance in Iraq: "The United Nations was feckless through the whole exercise. . . . Think about the fact that sanctions had been imposed and have been there since '91 and there have been a dozen Security Council resolutions Saddam Hussein had totally ignored. . . . Annan had taken the oil-for-food program that was set up for humanitarian purposes, totally corrupted it, turned it to his own purposes, making payments to high-ranking officials of governments with seats on the Security Council, and was actively and aggressively undermining this great international institution that was supposed to preserve world peace and keep Saddam in the bag. And [Saddam] owned them.

"The UN was a huge part of the problem . . . [especially because of] their failure to step up and enforce those resolutions throughout the '90s, to insist that he live up to the terms and conditions of the ceasefire of '91. So after we got in there and got set up, of course, [terrorists] hit the UN headquarters with a bomb, partly because [the UN] wouldn't allow us to render security [around the building]. Where I would say the UN was helpful was in setting up the elections process and working with us on it. They had credibility in certain circles."

It was Bremer who recruited the UN for the election role. And he used UN envoy Lakhdar Brahimi to persuade Ayatollah Sistani, the pro-democracy leader of Iraq's majority Shiites, that an election couldn't be held in short order. Bush regarded Bremer as his personal representative in Iraq. Bremer had been handpicked for the post as head of the Coalition Provisional Authority (CPA) by Rumsfeld, his deputy Paul Wolfowitz, and I. Lewis "Scooter" Libby, Cheney's chief of staff. The State Department went along, perhaps because of Bremer's close ties to former secretary of state Henry Kissinger. Bremer knew Bush's parents, but he'd never met the president before getting the Iraq post. Still, they hit it off instantly.

Roughly the same age, Bush and Bremer are alike in many ways. Both men came to serious religious faith relatively late in life, Bremer as a convert to Catholicism, Bush as a born-again Protestant. Both are family-oriented, immune to Washington's political games, and physical fitness buffs. Unlike many American diplomats, Bremer was not an Arabist. He did not look fondly on Arab despots. Bush thought that was an advantage. Like Bush, Bremer believed Arab countries were ripe for democracy. When Bremer was in Washington, he and Bush worked out together. The president said at a National Security Council meeting that he depended on Bremer for a candid assessment of the state of affairs in Iraq. "If Bremer's happy, I'm happy," Bush said. "If Bremer's nervous, I'm nervous. If Bremer's uneasy, I'm uneasy. If Bremer's optimistic, I'm optimistic."

Bremer, along with Rice, persuaded the president that financing the reconstruction of Iraq even partially by a loan would be a world-class mistake. Republicans on Capitol Hill, however, were clamoring to obligate Iraq for a large chunk of the expense. An Iraqi government, once elected, would have to pay off the loan through oil revenues, virtually its only source of income. And that, Bremer feared, would revive the specious idea that seizing Iraq's oil wealth was the secret motivation behind the invasion.

Months before, Rice had given Bush a copy of the book *Paris 1919* by historian Margaret MacMillan, the granddaughter of British prime minister David Lloyd George. The book gives a vivid account of the Versailles peace conference after World War I, at which Lloyd George and Georges Clemenceau, the French leader, agreed to punish Germany by imposing a huge fine that would take decades to pay off. This left the Germans with bitter feelings toward the allies who had defeated them—England, France, the United States. It impeded postwar reconciliation and contributed to the rise of Adolf Hitler and the outbreak of World War II in 1939.

The Versailles figure who interested Rice was President

Woodrow Wilson. He had vowed to reach a peace settlement that promoted freedom and self-determination but had failed notoriously to deliver on his promise. The book was "a very interesting story of pitfalls, of unclear objectives, of America not carrying through," Rice told me. "Versailles is one of the great missed opportunities in international history, which is why I thought it was a good thing to read." When Bremer also raised the Versailles parallel, Bush understood the lesson. With Bremer's help, he steered Republicans away from the loan option. Congress approved a $20 billion grant for Iraq.

To move toward democracy, Bremer and his CPA advisers devised a three-step scheme. It started with regional caucuses of leaders selected mostly by CPA officials and the Iraqi Governing Council, whose members had been appointed by Bremer. The caucuses would choose delegates to a convention assigned to draft an Iraqi constitution. That would be followed by an election of a legitimate, democratic government, after which the United States would hand over sovereignty.

There were two problems—big ones. Democracy came at the end of the process, not at the outset. And the Shiites, who make up more than 60 percent of Iraq's population, hated the arrangement. "The Shia were saying you cannot have unelected people write the constitution," Rice said. "There were people in the streets protesting for elections." Ayatollah Sistani persisted in calling for a national election. But Bremer didn't think the mechanism for an orderly election could be built soon enough to meet Sistani's impatient demand. Bush was unhappy over the impasse. He walked into a National Security Council meeting and asked, "How did we get on the wrong side of the issue of whether the Iraqis get to have elections? Now, how can it be that we are telling them they shouldn't have elections?"

Someone had to give. First it was Bremer and Rice, then Bush. The president was unbending on the goal of a democratic Iraq, but flexible on how to accomplish it. On a Sunday afternoon in November 2003, Bremer called Rice from Baghdad with a plan. She was at a Baltimore Ravens football game, but she carried a secure phone with her. Bremer outlined his new scheme. Rice recalled, "We knew that where we were [in bringing about democracy in Iraq] was not sustainable, and he had some ideas about how to change the course, and we decided that he really should come back and talk to the president." An hour later Bremer was on a plane for Washington. His wife, Francie, asked if he was going back to get fired. "No such luck," Bremer said.

Bush and Bremer dismissed another unhelpful French idea, this one to turn control of Iraq over to the appointed governing council. The president was worried about announcing a new timetable of events leading to democracy in Iraq. He didn't want to give the impression of incoherence and panic. Rather, he wanted a plan the American people could understand. Bremer's plan would change the sequence of steps toward democracy in Iraq. First an interim constitution would be drafted, then the United States would transfer sovereignty to a temporary government by June 30, 2004. That would be followed by a national election by the end of January 2005. The resulting transitional government would write a permanent constitution. Finally a new election would create a democratic government.

The plan was complicated, but the big steps—the hand-over and the January election—were clear. After those, the Iraqis would be in charge of everything except security. Bush sought assurance on the prime minister who would take over after the shift of sovereignty. Bush preferred a leader who would thank the United States for liberating Iraq and would work with the American military to fight the uprising by pro-Saddam diehards and jihadists. Bremer couldn't guarantee that, since the prime minister would be chosen by the governing council before it went out of business. Still, he influenced the selection of Iyad Allawi, a former exile who met Bush's specifications.

Bremer left to return to Baghdad. Before he departed, a story appeared in *USA Today* that the president had scolded Bremer over trouble in Iraq. Bush was miffed. He told his communications chief, Dan Bartlett, to call Bremer and reassure him of the White House's support. Bush had tried to show his backing for Bremer during their talks. At one point, he and Bremer had walked outdoors between the West Wing and the Eisenhower Executive Office Building. As TV cameras spotted them, Bush put his arm around Bremer. After sovereignty changed hands, Bremer returned to Washington and met with Bush. In the Oval Office, Bush gave Bremer a bear hug. He lifted Bremer's leg so a photographer could take a picture of the trademark boots Bremer wore in Iraq along with a blazer, a blue shirt, and a tie. Bush and Bremer spent nearly two hours sitting around the White House swimming pool and talking about Iraq and their religious faith. "I couldn't have made it in Iraq without my faith," Bremer told me.

AN AUDACIOUS PLAN

For Bush, the scheduled dates for the transfer of sovereignty and the first election were sacrosanct. Sticking to them, Bush felt, was important strategically. "He never wavered one time," Cheney told me. Bush feared that if the dates slipped, the Iraqis would become disillusioned. "He had an innate sense all along that the Iraqi people had to have reliable markers," Rice said, "that with all that was going on—violence and all of that—the political process was only going to keep moving forward by reliable markers." The president's "single most important decision" in Iraq, she told me, was to insist on sticking to the date of the election, January 30. He ignored predictions that the election would be chaotic and that terrorism would scare voters off. "They were just dead wrong," Cheney said. Because Bush didn't flinch, no one else did, either in Washington or inside Allawi's administration in Baghdad.

Bush's steadfastness produced further positive results. In October 2005, the Iraqi people went to the polls again, this time ratifying the constitution drafted by the parliament that had been elected in January. A robust 63 percent of eligible Iraqis voted. Of course, in the United States, the news of another successful election in Iraq was buried. The mainstream media instead played up the two-thousandth death of an American soldier in Iraq, a milestone that obscured the growing success of U.S. and Iraqi troops in combating the insurgency of Saddam's allies and foreign jihadists.

Bush flinched only once in Iraq. It was his most difficult decision of the postwar period. The issue was Fallujah, the city west of Baghdad filled with Sunni Muslim allies of Saddam and Islamic terrorists who had flooded into Iraq after the invasion. U.S. Marines had begun taking over the city in April 2004. But the cost in civilian casualties and political heartburn was high. The military wanted to continue the assault, if only to wipe out the chief staging area terrorists used for attacks all over Iraq. The commanding general, John Abizaid, "wanted to level the place," an American official told me. But Bremer was anxious to avert a political collapse. Two Iraqi cabinet ministers had resigned, Sunnis and even a few Shiites were ready to quit the governing council, and UN officials in Iraq to set up an election process were threatening to pull out. Bremer feared that the governing council would disintegrate and there would be no Iraqi government in place to accept sovereignty in June 2004. He urged Bush to order a pullback from Fallujah and wait until an Iraqi government was in charge. Bush agreed.

Seven months later, after Bush's reelection and with Allawi in charge of the interim Iraqi government, American troops returned to Fallujah and captured the city with minimal U.S. or civilian casualties. Nonetheless, a rare debate lingered at the White House over the initial decision to back off in Fallujah. A senior official who confers daily with the president told me, "I think Fallujah was a mistake." Bremer gave "bad advice," the official said. "A Bernard Lewis view of the war was much more accurate." Lewis, a professor emeritus at Princeton and a Middle East expert, had been a repeated guest at the White House to talk to Bush and his top advisers, and he argued that "what [the terrorists] respect is strength and toughness," the senior official said. According to this official, Lewis "believed that Fallujah was a direct attempt [by the insurgents] to re-create Mogadishu '93." Osama bin Laden himself had cited the pullout of American forces from Somalia following the infamous 1993 ambush of Army soldiers in Mogadishu as a sign of U.S. weakness. It emboldened al Qaeda terrorists to attack on 9/11, bin Laden said. According to Lewis's argument, the terrorists could have seen the American retreat from Fallujah as a sign of weakness, and that would have encouraged them to commit still more bloody acts of terrorism.

A question about Bush's foreign policy also remained: Why was he so bold and so willing to defy the foreign policy establishment and old allies, while his father was so restrained in comparison? Karl Rove, the president's chief political adviser, and other aides speak of Bush as the foreign policy heir of Presidents Truman and Reagan. These aides disregard the elder Bush. Rice, a foreign policy adviser to both Bushes, said the explanation is the times. The first President Bush had the task of "ending an era and harvesting the work of the fifty years before." His main job "was shepherding the Soviet Union along through its decline." He had to determine "whether to build NATO and whether or not to rearm Germany," Rice commented, but aside from deciding whether to expel Iraq from Kuwait in 1991, the elder Bush was not confronted with fundamental questions of war and peace. His son became president at "the start of this revolutionary period in the world where the old system is breaking down and where you have a new ideological challenge and you have to define a new world," she said. It's a more wide-open moment, like the era after World War II, and quite different from the times the elder Bush inherited.

But there was one audacious policy pursued by the elder Bush: instant reunification of democratic West Germany and Communist East Germany. "Nobody in the world thought that was the right answer" after the Berlin Wall came down in 1989, Rice recalled. "People thought, 'We'll have a process, maybe it'll be half in NATO, half in the Warsaw Pact.'" But the elder Bush decided unification must come "as fast as it can" and on West German terms. He staked out the American position and brought the British and French along. And unification occurred in a diplomatic blink of an eye. "It was very much the way George W. Bush would have made a decision about German unification."

Next to the pleasure of January 30, Bush enjoyed the day Saddam was captured in December 2003. He called Bremer in Baghdad and asked, "What's the reaction of the Iraqis?" Bremer told him about the coverage by al Jazeera, the Arab satellite news network that was consistently anti-American. A correspondent interviewed Iraqis in a long line to buy gasoline. To the chagrin of al Jazeera, the first interviewee was thrilled they'd grabbed Saddam. So were the second and third. Bush laughed and laughed.

Chapter 6

The Crusade for Democracy

THE BOOK BY NATAN SHARANSKY with the bland title, *The Case for Democracy*, came to President Bush in unbound galley form. It was sent by Tom Bernstein, a New York developer, a friend of Bush's at Yale, and later an investor in the Texas Rangers baseball team when Bush was an owner and managing general partner. Bernstein has an abiding interest in human rights and thought the book was so important the president ought to read it. Bush didn't read the galleys, but when an actual copy of the book arrived, just after the 2004 election, he dove in. A few days later, when he heard Sharansky was on a book tour in the United States, he asked an aide to invite Sharansky to the White House for a chat. The author, once a famous Russian dissident, now an Israeli, was reached in Philadelphia. He showed up at the White House the next day, nine days after Bush's reelection.

His first stop was the office of National Security Adviser Condoleezza Rice, soon to be secretary of state. "I'm reading your book, Natan," she told Sharansky. "Do you know why?

The president read it." Rice had dispatched an aide to a Borders bookstore near the White House when she learned Bush was reading the book. ("He reads five books for every one I read," Rice once confessed.) She and Sharansky talked about Rice's days as a foreign policy adviser in the elder Bush's administration, one less committed to spreading democracy and less friendly to Israel. "We chose stability over democracy and wound up with neither," she said. "Maybe if you choose democracy, you'll get both," Sharansky responded. That, of course, is a major theme of his book.

Sharansky spent an hour with Bush in the Oval Office. They were a mutual admiration society. Bush apologized for not having read the entire book. "I'm on page 210," he said. "I wanted to finish it last night but I fell asleep." He'd read the chapter criticizing his father's Middle East policy but hadn't gotten to the one in which Sharansky praises him. Sharansky had been thrilled in 2002 when Bush ostracized Yasser Arafat and urged Palestinians to establish a democratic government and elect new leaders. At the White House, Sharansky was accompanied by Ron Dermer, an Israeli diplomat who had helped him write the book. Both were impressed by Bush's humility. The president listened as Sharansky spelled out his ideas about democracy. They were mostly ideas Bush had already extolled in a series of speeches on democracy. Sharansky gave the president his highest accolade, likening him to the brave and persecuted champions of freedom in nondemocratic countries. "Mr. President, I see you as a dissident," he said. "Dissidents believe in an idea. They suffer a lot. But history proves them right."

That Bush and a Jewish exile from Russia who was now a member of the Israeli Knesset and Prime Minister Ariel Sharon's cabinet would get together, talk warmly, and agree wholeheartedly in a true meeting of the minds, on the eve of the president's second term—that could only happen if the Bush presidency had taken a radical turn. And indeed it had, splitting again with Bush's own State Department and the foreign policy establishment.

For months, Bush had dwelt on the subject of democracy in discussions with aides. Then, as a top priority of his second term, he took up a messianic mission to exert pressure for democracy around the world. Just one day after his reelection he made clear to speechwriter Michael Gerson that this mission would be his focus. "Let's get going on the inaugural address," the president told Gerson. "I want it to etch the Bush doctrine in stone."

Bush told the *New York Times* that Sharansky's view of democracy is "part of my presidential DNA. It's part of my philosophy." Maybe so, but the president revealed it only gradually. In his major campaign address on foreign policy five years earlier, he had promised a presidency that would be modest and humble in how it approached the world. In hindsight, one can see a hint of a strong commitment to democracy in that speech. But it was a hint no one, with the possible exception of Gerson and Bush himself, took seriously at the time. For sure, no one predicted that Bush would focus his second inaugural address—the speech the president had been so eager to begin writing—on this declaration: "It is the policy of the United States to seek and support the growth of democratic movements and institutions in every nation and culture, with the ultimate goal of ending tyranny in our world." Yet Bush said it, meant every breathtaking word of it, and soon was implementing it.

Bush's emphasis on democracy was not abstract. It was quite practical. In her Senate confirmation hearing for secretary of state, Rice seized on the most down-to-earth measure of freedom. "The world should apply what Natan Sharansky calls the 'town square test': if a person cannot walk into the middle of the town square and express his or her views without fear of arrest, imprisonment, or physical harm, then that person is living in a fear society, not a free society," Rice said. "We cannot rest until every person living in a fear society has finally won their freedom." Within weeks, she was in Belarus, which the Bush administration had dubbed the least democratic country in Europe, meeting with dissidents and encouraging them to keep up their struggle for democracy. For his part, Bush forced Russian president Vladimir Putin to talk about democracy at their press conference after a one-on-one meeting in Slovakia. Putin looked unhappy, but he said Russia would not turn back from democracy to a Communist dictatorship.

For Bush, the sensitive part of the drive for democracy was that it put the United States at odds with longtime allies such as Egypt and Saudi Arabia and former adversaries that had become friendlier—Russia, for example. It was easy to call out Cuba, North Korea, Syria, Myanmar, Zimbabwe, and Iran for their lack of democracy. Their relations with America were either bad or nonexistent. There was no diplomatic heartburn if Bush zinged them by name. But after the 9/11 terrorist attacks, the president couldn't ignore the fact that the nineteen perpetrators came from Saudi Arabia and Egypt, both countries that crush dissent but permit anti-American sentiment to flourish. The easy way out for Bush would have been to cite the broad Middle East as the problem, not a particular country. Bush didn't take it. He believes tyrannies produce terrorists but democracies don't. So in a 2003 speech to the National Endowment for Democracy, Bush gingerly prodded Saudi Arabia and Egypt toward democracy. "By giving the Saudi people a greater role in their own society, the Saudi government can demonstrate true leadership in the region," he said. "The great and proud country of Egypt . . . should show the way toward democracy in the Middle East."

The president has made the Middle East the top priority on his democracy agenda—first Afghanistan, on the fringe of the region; then Iraq; now the others. Bush and Rice didn't take it lightly when Egyptian president Hosni Mubarak jailed Ayman Nour, who had vowed to challenge Mubarak in the 2005 presidential election. Mubarak was used to running Saddam Hussein–style: without an opponent. At Rice's instruction, the State Department condemned the arrest and called Nour "one of Egypt's most prominent opposition leaders." Then Rice conferred with Egyptian foreign minister Ahmed Gheit and told him the Nour arrest threatened to harm U.S.-Egypt relations. She might reconsider a planned visit to Egypt, Rice said, unless Nour was released. Gheit offered excuses. At a press conference, Rice made her private complaint public. When Nour was not released from jail, Rice canceled the trip. In a matter of days, Egypt caved to the U.S. pressure and released Nour.

A CLEAR MESSAGE

To understand Bush's fixation on democracy, you have to know his unusual approach to drafting speeches. Bush believes speeches are enormously important for two reasons. One, effective presidential leadership requires speeches that attract attention and make a point. Two, speeches can drive policy. Bush thought his father's presidency was diminished by the absence of memorable words to explain and celebrate the end of the Cold War. The elder Bush's most famous phrases came during the 1988 campaign ("kinder, gentler" and "Read my lips, no new taxes"), not during his presidency. Bush has reversed that. More important, he has used his presidential speeches to advance policies far beyond where his aides expected him to go. Rather than reflect policy, his speeches dictate policy. He teased Rice about what he might say in his second inaugural address. "You're not going to believe what I say," he told her. "I hope I get to see it before you give it," Rice responded. What she and other senior Bush advisers later saw was a near-final draft to which only minor changes could be made. The thrust of the speech—the new direction, the policy declaration—had been set.

Two people play the key role in Bush speeches: the president and Michael Gerson. This is different from how other presidents have worked. President Truman's famous speech in which he laid out the "Truman doctrine" of blocking Communist expansion was written at the State Department and merely edited at the White House. President Reagan's speeches were drafted weeks beforehand and circulated for comment among senior officials. Bitter fights ensued over what should be left in or edited out. The State Department sought to erase the most riveting line from Reagan's 1987 speech at the Berlin Wall, "Mr. Gorbachev, tear down this wall." Queasy officials censored Reagan's reference to the Soviet Union as an "evil empire," only to see it crop up months later in another Reagan speech. President Clinton got involved late in the speechmaking process. He tinkered with speeches until the last possible moment. Clinton continued editing one of his State of the Union speeches as he rode in his limousine to the Capitol. Bush regarded the Clinton process as disorderly.

Bush's speeches reflect the close collaboration between the president and Gerson, a relationship that goes back to 1999. Then a candidate for president, Bush summoned Gerson to his hotel room in Washington when he was attending a governor's conference. The Texas governor had never met Gerson. (In fact, Karl Rove, Bush's political adviser, thought Bush had called in *Mark* Gerson, a young neoconservative.) But Bush's press secretary, Karen Hughes, had researched Gerson's speeches, indeed his whole career. Gerson had written speeches for the likes of Chuck Colson, Congressman Jack Kemp, Bill Bennett after his stint as education secretary, and Senator Dan Coats. And based on that background, he became Bush's first and only choice for speechwriter. In that first meeting, Bush was blunt: he offered Gerson the job on the spot. At the time, he knew about Gerson's strong religious faith, but not about his passionate feelings on spreading democracy. The speechwriter turned out to be completely in sync with Bush on both subjects. Indeed, many of Gerson's own ideas have made their way into speeches on democracy and Bush's faith-based initiative.

Hughes was initially disappointed in the speeches Gerson drafted for Bush, fearing they didn't capture Bush's style of communicating. She was wrong. Gerson gave Bush what he needed most, a presidential voice. And he became a trusted adviser. After 9/11, Gerson joined the president at Camp David to draft the announcement of military action in Afghanistan. As he wrote, Bush was giving military orders on a secure phone. Suddenly, Bush put his hand over the phone and asked Gerson, "Do you have a security clearance?" Gerson said he didn't think so. "You do now," the president declared.

Typically, the Bush speechwriting process begins with a meeting between the president and Gerson, in which Bush presents what he wants to say and Gerson contributes a long list of his own ideas. After the initial meeting, a speech is drafted by Gerson and his associates, particularly John McConnell. For his second term, Bush elevated Gerson to the job of counselor and named Bill McGurn, a former *Wall Street Journal* editorial writer, as chief speechwriter. But Gerson still plays a role in major speeches. Once drafted, a speech is circulated but it is not open to debate. This is the first time most White House and administration officials see a speech. It already has the president's imprimatur. Advisers are free to recommend a change in wording, but Bush does not tolerate attempts to alter the general direction of a speech. He is informed of every edit, no matter how tiny. In his speeches on democracy, Bush was steadily pushing a policy forward. "The president says what he wants to say," an aide told me. "The policy details have to catch up and reflect this."

There's a saying in Washington that if you want to know what Bush is thinking, read the speeches. In interviews and press conferences, the president is often rambling and opaque. In speeches, he is precise and clear. Bush likes surprises, but he doesn't indulge in trickery or misdirection. If his words point in a particular direction, that's the direction he is surely headed in. This was true in his speeches on Iraq, Social Security reform, and Medicare. It was especially true on democracy. In speeches starting in 1999, one could see the centerpiece of Bush's foreign policy, his commitment to democracy, grow and flower, its fullest expression coming in the second inaugural. "That second inaugural was pure George Bush," Cheney told me. "It's been building for four years."

Along the way, Bush developed at least ten separate themes, most of them anathema to the supposed wise men and women of the foreign ministries and foreign policy establishments of the United States and Europe. The ten, in which Bush often uses the words *freedom*, *liberty*, and *democracy* interchangeably, are:

1. America's overriding mission in the world is to champion freedom.
2. Democracy is for everyone in every country at all times, and it is condescending to think otherwise.
3. America doesn't bestow democracy, God does.
4. The unmistakable direction of history is toward freedom.

5. Democracy is the best weapon against terrorism.
6. The pursuit of freedom produces the goals of foreign policy idealists and realists—democracy, security, and stability.
7. Democracy leads to peace among nations.
8. The best place to seek a democratic revolution is the Middle East.
9. America and Europe bear a large measure of the blame for the absence of democracy in the Middle East.
10. A campaign for liberty has the best chance of succeeding if the United States leads.

In his 2000 presidential campaign, Bush's first two mentions of freedom and democracy encapsulated many of these themes without elaborating on them. Bush, with Gerson's help, knew exactly what his policy should be and what it would produce. A single sentence in his 1999 campaign autobiography, *A Charge to Keep*, touched on freedom. The book, largely ignored at the time, was ghostwritten by Karen Hughes, one of Bush's closest advisers. "Our greatest export is freedom, and we have a moral obligation to champion it throughout the world," it said.

Bush went further in the most important foreign policy speech of his campaign, delivered just before the primaries. "Some have tried to pose a choice between American ideals and American interests, between who we are and how we act," Bush said. "But the choice is false. America, by decision and destiny, promotes political freedom and gains the most when democracy advances." These two sentences drew little attention and provoked no controversy. Looking back, we see that what Bush said then was unusually predictive of what he would declare as U.S. policy later. But it wouldn't be until the second inaugural that Bush would give full expression to the notion that the pursuit of democracy linked idealists and realists. In the campaign speech, that idea was drowned out by Bush's stress on stability rather than freedom. "Generations of democratic peace" would be "accomplished by concentrating on enduring national interests," he said. "And these are my priorities."

Next, after the campaign address, came Bush's first inaugural address, and it didn't create momentum for a crusade for democracy either. His words were forgettable. "Through much of the last century, America's faith in freedom and democracy was a rock in raging seas," he said. "Now it is a seed upon the wind, taking root in many nations. Our democratic faith is more than the creed of our country. It is the inborn hope of humanity, an ideal we carry but do not own, a trust we bear and pass along." Nine months later, however, there was an intervening event—9/11. "The key elements [of the democracy policy] were in place—the rapid expansion of liberty in recent decades and the fact that liberty is the design of nature," a White House official told me. "But the events of September 11 provided an urgency to those views, and there was an opportunity to advance liberty in a way that was not possible prior to September 11."

The president used his State of the Union speech early in 2002 to nail down his concern for democracy, starting in the Middle East. The Middle East section of the speech was, in the president's mind, the most critical. He and his aides were certain the press would leap on his urgent call for democracy in the Middle East. Rice had called Egyptian and Saudi leaders to give them a heads-up on remarks they wouldn't like. "Look," she recalled telling them, "you're going to hear this and, you know, we're not trying to finger anybody, but this is important to the president." Rice also provided a background briefing for reporters a few hours before the speech and emphasized the pitch for democracy in the Middle East. But something else grabbed the media's attention and dominated the news and the commentary. Bush had labeled Iraq, Iran, and North Korea an "axis of evil."

Nonetheless, his words on democracy mattered. "We have no intention of imposing our culture," he said. "But America will always stand firm for the nonnegotiable demands of human dignity, the rule of law, limits on the power of the state, respect for women, private property, free speech, equal justice, and religious tolerance. America will take the side of brave men and women who advocate these values around the world, including the Islamic world." That meant the Middle East. Bush went on to proclaim a more ambitious goal than thwarting terrorists. "We have a greater objective than eliminating threats and containing resentment," he said. "We seek a just and peaceful world beyond the war on terror."

Bush had a lot more to say on the subject, and he used a speech just before the invasion of Iraq to begin saying it. The event was the annual dinner of the American Enterprise Institute, the respected conservative think tank. The president underscored one point: democracy is a universal aspiration, applicable everywhere, including Iraq. "It is presumptuous and insulting to suggest that a whole region of the world—the one-fifth of humanity that is Muslim—is somehow untouched by the most basic aspirations of life," Bush said. "Human cultures can be vastly different. Yet the human heart desires the same good thing. . . . Freedom and democracy will always and everywhere have a greater appeal than the slogans of hatred and the tactics of terror." Bush reminded his audience that many once saw Japan and Germany as "incapable of sustaining democratic values. Well, they were wrong. Some say the same of Iraq today. They are mistaken. The nation of Iraq is fully capable of moving toward democracy and living in freedom." Bush was at least partially right. The dazzling success of the Iraqi election on January 30, 2005, vindicated his optimism.

In late 2003, Bush propelled his democracy campaign another step forward. Celebrating the twentieth anniversary of the National Endowment for Democracy, he said the historical trend favors freedom. "Over time, free nations grow stronger and dictatorships grow weaker," Bush insisted. And America's influence is obvious, he said: "It is no accident that the rise of so many democracies took place in a time when the world's most influential nation was itself a democracy." Bush said freedom is not only "worth fighting for, dying for, and standing for," it "leads to peace." Now, he said, "we must apply that lesson in our own time. We've reached another great turning point, and the resolve we show will shape the next stage of the world democratic movement." He listed targets for freedom: the Middle East, particularly Iran, Egypt, and Saudi Arabia; China; all Islamic countries; the Palestinians.

But the eye-popping part of his speech was a condemnation of America and Europe. "Sixty years of Western nations' excusing and accommodating the lack of freedom in the Middle East did nothing to make us safe, because in the long run stability cannot be purchased at the expense of liberty," he said. This was an indictment of ten administrations, including that of the elder Bush and the early months of his own. "As long as the Middle East remains a place where freedom does not flourish, it will remain a place of stagnation, resentment, and violence ready to export," he said. It would be "reckless to accept the status quo" in the Middle East, Bush said, and he hasn't. Following Iraq's election, he pressured Syria to withdraw its troops from Lebanon and exerted pressure for free elections in Egypt and Lebanon.

Bush followed up on this theme in a speech in England two weeks later. "We must shake off decades of failed policy in the Middle East," he stated. But his emphasis was on what he dubbed a "pillar" of security, "the global expansion of democracy." The more democracy, the less terrorism, he said. "In democratic and successful societies, men and women do not swear allegiance to malcontents and murderers," Bush declared. "They turn their hearts and labor to building better lives. And democratic governments do not shelter terrorists or attack their peaceful neighbors." In fighting terror and tyranny, he said, "we have an unmatched advantage, a power than cannot be resisted and that is the appeal of freedom to all mankind."

All Bush's themes were tied together in his second inaugural address. Everything he'd implied or suggested was made explicit. The speech shocked Washington. It caught the press, the political community, and the city's establishment totally off-guard. Even after four years of the Bush presidency, they hadn't figured the man out. They anticipated a conventional speech, conciliatory and maybe a bit complacent, stressing his domestic program and steadfastness in Iraq and the war on terror. Instead, Bush's message was: *You ain't seen nothin' yet.* Rather than relaxing and settling for modest aims, he called for a bold, unrelenting crusade for democracy. Bush knew most of the press and the old foreign policy hands would hate the speech. He didn't care. He hadn't come to Washington to please the town but to change it.

The speech was an extraordinary tribute to freedom. When Bush's other speeches are forgotten, compelling as several of them were, this one will be remembered. It was succinct and sweeping. The idealist and realist strains were united. "The survival of liberty in our land increasingly depends on the success of liberty in other lands," Bush said. "America's vital interests and our deepest beliefs are now one." He took a swipe at doubters who "have questioned the global appeal of liberty." Americans, of all people, "should never be surprised by the power of our ideals." Bush, for one, never is.

Natan Sharansky watched the Bush inaugural speech on TV in Israel. Thanks to Bush, his book had gone international. Bush gave a copy to Tony Blair and urged other world leaders to read it. When Blair held a conference in London on Israel and the Palestinians, he sounded as if he'd read it. He had been criticized for the Israelis' failure to show up. Not a problem, he said. The issue was democracy, and those who needed it were the Palestinians. Sharansky choked up when he heard Bush's words. They were his and Bush's, melded eloquently. "I was deeply moved by the speech," Sharansky told me. "My only regret is Andrei Sakharov didn't live to hear this speech." Sakharov, the scientist behind the Soviet hydrogen bomb, was the father of the democracy movement in Russia and Sharansky's mentor. Sakharov would have loved every word.

Chapter 7

Taking Ownership

PRESIDENT BUSH DOESN'T KNOW where the phrase came from, but he doesn't think he swiped it from someone. Karl Rove doesn't know either, nor does his aide Peter Wehner, who keeps track of everything Bush says. Speechwriter Michael Gerson hasn't the foggiest idea of the origin of the phrase.

Whatever the source, the first time the president uttered the words *ownership* and *society* in close proximity was during his presidential campaign in 2000. In an interview on CNN, Bush defended his plan for using Social Security payroll taxes to fund individual investment accounts. "They will give people the security of ownership," he said. "Ownership in our society should not be an exclusive club."

Of course, Republicans have long regarded ownership as a conservative virtue. But before Bush, they concentrated more on what leads to ownership: opportunity. Back in the early 1980s a group of congressional Republicans led by a young Georgia congressman named Newt Gingrich began calling itself the Conservative Opportunity Society. But it was Bush who took the next step and made ownership a broad new political theme.

Since he did so, the phrase *ownership society* could some-day enter the lexicon of presidential trademarks. Franklin D. Roosevelt had the New Deal, John F. Kennedy the New Frontier, Lyndon B. Johnson the Great Society. Now the Ownership Society has come to represent a new direction in domestic policy designed to encourage citizens to become more self-reliant, responsible, and free of dependence on government. It goes against the grain of more than seventy years of national policy. FDR, JFK, and LBJ expanded the supply of government. Ronald Reagan briefly and unsuccessfully sought to reduce the supply, as did conservatives in Congress in the early days of the "Republican Revolution" of the mid-1990s. Bush would ease the *demand* for government by letting individuals decide how to save, invest, and handle their health care expenses. He would do it by transforming Social Security and Medicare, creating new and attractive retirement accounts, increasing home ownership, and reforming the tax code.

The creation of an ownership society is Bush's most radical policy and the most difficult to enact. His pursuit of democracy around the world isn't nearly as groundbreaking. Past presidents have sought to spread democracy, just not with as much fortitude, vigor, and indifference to political sensitivities as Bush. Granted, Bush's overturning of the policy presidents had followed in the Middle East for a half-century was bold. But it hasn't affected the lives of Americans as tangibly as a true ownership society would. What Bush has proposed is a fundamental shift in power from the federal government and bureaucrats in Washington to individual Americans. It's not to be confused with federalism, which involves the sharing of power between the national and state governments. That's an idea that goes back to the founding of the country. There's no single word for Bush's brainchild. Thus Bush had to come up with one himself.

By 2002, "ownership society" was slipping into his speeches with regularity. "I want America to be an ownership society," he told the National Summit on Retirement Savings that year, "a society where a life of work becomes a life of retirement." At the time, his "ownership society" was not a full-blown program. It had only one element, personal investment accounts using Social Security taxes. At least this was the only one he talked up. Health accounts and expanded home ownership were already Bush initiatives, but he hadn't yet packaged them with Social Security reform in a single program. Bush came to regard the phrase "ownership society" affectionately. He didn't bother to test it beforehand in a poll or with focus groups.

To promote the cause of ownership, the president would simultaneously decrease and increase the federal government's role. Bush, of course, is a pro-government conservative who would use Washington in areas—education and marriage, to name two—that many conservatives prefer to leave to the states. To build an ownership society, he would take away some of the federal government's authority over investments of payroll taxes and over health care. Not only would the government have less tax revenue to manage and spend, it would yield a significant amount of control over the Social Security and Medicare systems themselves. But to expand home ownership, Bush would shift power the other way. Picking up on a program that President Clinton never implemented, he has enlarged the job of the government in directing federal subsidies to minorities and low-income homeowners. On balance, however, Washington would have far less power.

Though Bush hasn't given a major speech on the subject, he does have a vision of the cultural impact of an ownership society. "I think part of government's responsibility is to encourage certain cultures," he told me. "And a primary cultural change that I have been trying to instill ever since I got into public office" is a new "period of personal responsibility." Ownership "does a lot of things," Bush said. "One of the things ownership does is it helps foster personal accountability." This includes "independence from government. Government sometimes, because you're dependent on it, undermines the sense of personal responsibility."

Ownership also gives people "a vital stake in our country," he said. "If you own something, it's more likely that you'll say, 'Well, gosh, I've got a vital stake in the future. I've got the sense of ownership.' . . . There's a direct link between participation and ownership, participation and democracy and ownership." Bush tied the ownership society to his notion of compassionate conservatism. "The compassionate conservative promotes ownership and the compassionate conservative recognizes there are some who cannot help themselves. And it's that combination of helping the poor, coupled with encouraging people not to remain poor and to have that dream of owning something, that makes this philosophy a much more optimistic philosophy."

The notion of ownership as the theme for the boldest elements of Bush's domestic policy has a long and odd history. Bush has been an advocate of reforming Social Security and allowing individuals to use their payroll taxes to invest in private accounts since a speech at a Texas country club in 1978. When he announced his presidential campaign in Amana, Iowa, in 1999, he said establishing private accounts in Social Security was one of his top three goals. But he made no mention of an "ownership society." Nor did he when, midway into his first term, the Treasury Department developed a new type of individual retirement account that would permit participants to deposit up to $7,500 a year and remove funds early without a penalty. In 2003, as part of a compromise that won congressional approval of a Medicare prescription drug benefit, Bush gained a significant expansion of health savings accounts. These give individuals discretion in routine medical decisions, including when to see doctors and how much to pay them. Once more, though, it wasn't designated as part of a larger package. Meanwhile, the home ownership initiative was humming along, exceeding Bush's goal for minority home purchases. Bush also promised in 2004 to seek to overhaul the entire federal tax code, and he set up a commission to make recommendations.

Finally, as Bush campaigned for reelection, these five initiatives emerged as a package, a cleverly conceived package.

Together, Social Security private accounts, "lifetime" IRAs, health accounts, tax reform, and the home ownership program became the "ownership society." And later, after Hurricane Katrina, Bush injected elements of ownership in his recovery plan for the Gulf Coast, including the parceling out of federal land to those willing to build (and own) houses on it.

There's no reason for Bush to be embarrassed by the jerry-built nature of the program. That's the way Roosevelt's New Deal came together: separate programs tied in a bundle with a name attached. There was a thread running through FDR's scheme: big government in Washington as the answer to America's economic and social problems. And there's an idea that unites Bush's package: individuals acting responsibly, not big government in Washington, is the answer.

Bush adviser Karl Rove was enthusiastic about the package, regarding it as an agenda for the future and a political winner. Its most controversial element was reform of Social Security. Most of Washington wasn't interested in reform and, indeed, looked askance at tinkering with Social Security. Bush's own staff was divided. And in Congress, nearly all Democrats and many Republicans—House Majority Leader Tom DeLay, for one—didn't want to touch Social Security. Yet in a typical display of his "rebel-in-chief" style, Bush decided to go ahead with the full, ambitious reform plan. There would be no small-ball. And he had talked up the Social Security reform plan during the campaign without committing political suicide. That might have been, in part, because Democrats didn't have a forward-looking agenda of their own, but it also could have been because he presented his ideas on Social Security in the context of this larger reform package, the "ownership society." Once the overhaul of Social Security became a real possibility rather than a campaign talking point, of course, it faced lockstep Democratic opposition and dwindling public support.

In his acceptance speech at the 2004 Republican convention, Bush said, "Another priority for a new term is to build an ownership society, because ownership brings security and dignity and independence." He set a goal of 7 million more "affordable homes" over the next decade, "so more American families will be able to open the door and say, 'Welcome to my home.'" And "in an ownership society, more people will own their own health plans and have the confidence of owning a piece of their retirement." Bush said private accounts would be "a nest egg you can call your own and government can never take away."

In case anyone thought the "ownership society" was mere window dressing, Bush disabused them of this notion in his second inaugural address. "To give every American a stake in the promise and future of our country . . . we will build an ownership society," he declared. "We will widen the ownership of homes and businesses, retirement savings and health insurance, preparing our people for the challenge of life in a free society." And every American, he said, would become "an agent of his or her own destiny."

Though the president had forcefully laid out a bold agenda for his second term, Republicans on Capitol Hill remained reluctant to touch the third rail of American politics. The job of pioneering the way to reform was left to Bush.

"The members are willing to do this," House majority whip Roy Blunt told the president, but "they're not willing to be the scouts." In other words, they'd vote for Social Security reform but not put their necks on the line campaigning for it. That would have to be the president's job. Bush said he knew that. So he threw his weight behind pushing his plan.

Indeed, he devoted the first half of 2005 to touring the country to tout Social Security reform and the virtues of ownership. It was a solo tour, of course. He spoke at dozens of town hall meetings and gave numerous speeches to make his case directly to the American people. "Personal accounts are critical to building an ownership society," he said in Columbia, South Carolina, "a more optimistic and more hopeful America, in which more people own their own homes, more people own their own businesses, more people have an ownership in a retirement account, more people have an asset base they call their own that they can pass on to whomever they choose." In Cedar Rapids, Iowa, the president insisted that ownership shouldn't be confined to members of an investor class. "That's not what I think," he said. "I think the more investors we have, the more owners we have in America, the better off America is." In Tucson, Arizona, he said, "I think if you own something, you have a vital stake in the future of the country. I think we ought to encourage ownership throughout America."

With little encouragement from Republicans in Congress, Bush was taking on the combined forces of the Democratic Party, well-heeled liberal groups, organized labor, and AARP, the powerful special interest group claiming to represent

America's elderly. Democrats in Congress pressured their members against joining Bush's reform drive or even offering an alternative. Only a single Democratic congressman, Alan Boyd of Florida, ventured forward to cosponsor a Social Security reform bill. When Bush summoned members of Congress to the White House to discuss his proposals, he was animated. He inched to the edge of his chair as he spoke. He was "literally forward-leaning," Roy Blunt told me.

Despite the political opposition he faced, Bush's passion wasn't irrational. Propelling the formation of an ownership society was a revolution America had undergone in how its citizens save for retirement and invest. The revolution began in the early 1980s with President Reagan's deep tax cuts and the expansion of IRA and 401(k) savings plans. These brought about two big changes. Employers abandoned pensions in favor of giving direct contributions to a retirement fund for each employee known for its section in the tax code, 401(k). On their own, millions of middle-class Americans invested the funds in their individual retirement accounts. The second change was the emergence of a burgeoning investor class of people who never before had owned financial assets. Stock ownership grew from 20 percent of Americans in 1983 to 52 percent in 2001. Bush envisioned 80 percent of Americans as stockholders in an ownership society. Addressing a rally in Tampa shortly after his second inauguration, the president said, "I like the concept of people getting a quarterly statement about how their stocks and bonds are doing in their own personal account. Now some of you are glazing over. I understand. Think about private property in an account that . . .

earns a better return than the current system and you'll end up with more money."

There was also a philosophical case for ownership. As far back as the seventeenth century, the British political thinker John Locke suggested that owning property benefited society. "He who appropriates land to himself by his labor does not lessen but increase the common stock of mankind," Locke wrote in his *Second Treatise of Government*. It was Locke's writing that inspired Thomas Jefferson and the Founders to proclaim in the Declaration of Independence the right to "life, liberty, and the pursuit of happiness." When Alexis de Tocqueville visited America in the 1830s, he commented on the virtue of widespread ownership of property. "As a man is made aware of the price of things and he discovers that he can be stripped of his in his turn, he becomes more circumspect and ends by respecting in those like him what he wants to be respected in himself," he wrote.

George W. Bush's administration has also made more practical cases for ownership. A scholarly study by the Consumer Federation of America discovered in 2003 that paying off a mortgage on a home is "the easiest way for lower income and minority households to build personal wealth." Another study found that children whose parents own a home are more likely to graduate from high school, go to college, and get a college degree.

Then there is the example from British prime minister Margaret Thatcher in the 1980s. Thatcher sold public housing units to residents and privatized government-run industries. The British economy soared. "The Thatcherite argues that being one's own master—in the sense of owning one's own home or disposing of one's own property—provides an incentive to think differently about the world," wrote political philosopher Shirley Robin Letwin in *The Anatomy of Thatcherism*. Letwin added, "Nor is it only independence and self-sufficiency which the Thatcherite hopes to encourage by means of wider ownership. Personal energy and adventurousness, critical components of the vigorous virtues . . . are also believed by the Thatcherite to be encouraged by wider ownership."

Bush hasn't been quite that extravagant in his claims for ownership, but White House aides have come close. "Ownership contributes to community," said Peter Wehner in a speech to the Hudson Institute, a Washington think tank. "When people own their own houses, they become vested not just in their property, but their community. It makes people more communally responsible. Ownership also elicits greater commitment and care from owners themselves. In the history of the world, it's been said, nobody ever washed a rented car." Similarly, a White House paper argued, "Ownership brings security and dignity and independence. We seek not just government programs but a path to greater opportunity, more freedom, and more control over your own life."

DEMAND-SIDE CONSERVATISM

It was as a young Republican candidate for Congress from west Texas that Bush first spoke favorably about Social Security reform. He addressed a crowd of Realtors at the Midland

Country Club and rashly predicted that Social Security would be broke in ten years. (It took fifteen years—and imminent bankruptcy was averted only because in 1983 the age of eligibility for retirement benefits was raised and the ceiling on income subject to payroll taxation was lifted.) "The ideal option would be for Social Security to be made sound and people be given the chance to invest the money the way they feel," Bush said. He was talking up the same idea, private investment accounts, that would become the heart of his "ownership society" decades later.

Otherwise, though, Bush didn't make much of the issue during the 1978 campaign. In fact, his Democratic opponent, Kent Hance, doesn't recall the issue being raised at all. (Hance won that election, and as a congressman he cosponsored the Reagan tax cut bill in 1981. He later became a Republican and a Bush supporter. Now a lobbyist, he was invited to a White House reception after Bush's second inaugural. When he approached the receiving line of Bush and Vice President Dick Cheney, the president bellowed, "Kent Hance!" Turning to Cheney, he said, "Dick, we wouldn't be here if it wasn't for this guy." Cheney said he knew that. "I'd be chairman of the House Agriculture Committee now," Bush said. "And you'd have real power," Hance shot back.)

In the 1990s, as a Texas governor with an eye on the presidency, Bush revived his interest in Social Security. Rove, the strategist in his successful campaign in 1994, brought a series of experts to Austin to confer with Bush on the subject. Among them was former Swedish prime minister Carl Bildt, an architect of Sweden's reformed retirement system, which now has private accounts. (Rove had met Bildt in his college Republican days, at a gathering of young European and American conservatives.) José Piñera, who set up Chile's plan, also with individual accounts, dropped by to chat with Bush. So did Harvard professor Martin Feldstein, an expert on the economic effects of Social Security. By 1998, when Bush consulted economists who would advise him in the presidential campaign, he'd made up his mind in favor of individual accounts and talked about them during the 2000 race. But it wasn't until his reelection that he was ready to mount a serious effort to pressure Congress to approve the accounts.

The accounts are largely the basis for the description of Bush as a demand-side conservative. Over the past two and a half decades, conservatives had controlled the White House or Congress, or both, and yet failed to cut the size and scope of government. Their mistake was to go after the supply of government, according to Republican national chairman Ken Mehlman. Each program or agency has a lobby in Washington that supports it relentlessly, making meaningful cuts all but impossible, even for Ronald Reagan and Newt Gingrich. Through private accounts and other ownership society reforms, however, Bush would reduce the demand for government. Those who opt for a private account would get smaller Social Security benefits, just as Medicare beneficiaries using health savings accounts would require a smaller government subsidy. That's the theory, anyway.

As appealing as the idea of an ownership society might be, it clashed with the liberal sense of what a social safety net should be. Liberals prefer defined benefits—not investment accounts or health savings accounts—to be guaranteed by Social Security, Medicaid, and Medicare. In other words, no reform and no change. This puts liberals athwart the private sector revolution on pensions and health benefits. In both cases, employers have turned to fixed sums of money to be given to employees for retirement and health accounts. The employees determine how to invest the retirement money and how to spend on medical care. Liberals don't want to leave even part of the safety net to individuals in the three biggest public programs.

Liberals see the clash over Bush's plan to expand ownership at the expense of government in stark philosophical terms. Ownership, they believe, leads inevitably to inequality. Only government, especially through Social Security, can make society more equitable. And there's an emotional reason for their opposition. Social Security is the crown jewel of liberal programs, associated with the heyday of liberal Democratic ascendancy in the 1930s. Tinkering with it, much less overhauling it totally, instantly brings liberals to the barricades, as Bush discovered to his dismay.

So the struggle over reform was a titanic one. But imagine if the president had won the fight for private accounts in Social Security. And imagine if he had expanded consumer-driven health care by giving individuals a tax deduction for the full cost of a high-deductible insurance policy that is linked to a health savings account covering everyday medical expenses. Imagine further that he had gained congressional approval of lifetime IRAs and tax reform that lowers individual income tax

rates. Imagine also that minority home ownership had continued to exceed expectations because of aid from the federal
program Bush has backed aggressively. All of which was possible. Achieving it would have been an epic feat. And Bush,
having succeeded in creating an ownership society, would be
the most important and consequential domestic policy president since FDR.

By itself, Bush's decision to tackle Social Security and fight
for an ownership society reflected an audacious governing
style. On Social Security, he chose the extreme option, the
most controversial and least likely to pass. He was contemptuous of proposing anything less ambitious, anything modest or
smacking of small-ball. He would challenge the Washington
wisdom that sweeping reform was impossible. He would leave
his mark on Washington not by shrinking government, as
conventional conservatives would, but by reforming it and letting individuals decide how to spend the tax dollars aimed at
helping them. So he chose the risky over the prosaic and the
safe. This was the mark of a unique president.

And one day, either on his watch or a subsequent president's, when America becomes an ownership society, he will
be vindicated.

Chapter 8

Faith-Based

Senator Eugene McCarthy, a wit and a Catholic, said only two kinds of religion are permissible in Washington: either strong beliefs, vaguely expressed, or vague beliefs, strongly expressed. George W. Bush falls into a third category. His religion consists of strong beliefs, strongly affirmed. This was bound to lead to trouble, especially since Bush has never been reticent about discussing religion.

"The president's faith," White House speechwriter Michael Gerson told me, "is close to the surface and comes out easily, unself-consciously." As governor of Texas, Bush was told a reporter wanted to interview him about his faith. When the reporter showed up, Bush started talking about how he became an evangelical Christian even before the reporter had asked a single question. After his first hundred days in the White House, he sat down for a series of TV interviews. When Fox News anchor Brit Hume asked the president whether he would answer a few questions about his faith, Bush agreed, saying, "Those will be the most important questions I get all day." Returning on Air Force One from the funeral of Pope

John Paul II in April 2005, Bush got into a conversation with reporters about Christianity and doubts. "I think a walk in faith constantly confronts doubt, as faith becomes more mature," he said. But "my faith is strong." Later Bush volunteered additional thoughts on the subject of doubt. "There is no doubt in my mind there is a living God," he said. "And no doubt in my mind that the Lord, Christ, was sent by the Almighty."

Bush has the same Christian faith as millions of Americans. But it's a faith that sets him apart from most of America's political class. It's not Sundays-only Christianity. It's more intense and demanding—and, in a secular era, more likely to annoy nonbelievers. Gerson, a student of Christian theology, said Bush "comes from the small-group evangelical movement, a kind of 'Mere Christianity,' as C. S. Lewis called it, that focuses on a personal relationship with God." His faith is rooted in his own experience. He reached a crisis in his life at age forty, embraced Jesus Christ as his personal savior in a serious way, and soon found that his life had changed for the better. This is a common experience among Christians who come to faith, or to true faith, as adults. Bush prays frequently during the day, sometimes in the Oval Office. He reads a daily devotional and the Bible. He is not a Bible literalist. He doesn't have a problem with evolution. He has little interest in theology or eschatology. And he hasn't bothered to read the popular Christian books on prophecy and the end times by Tim LaHaye, the Left Behind series.

The president meets often with Christian leaders such as Charles Colson of Prison Fellowship and Rick Warren, author of the best-selling *The Purpose-Driven Life*. The meetings are private, thus not included on Bush's public schedule. Journalist Ron Suskind wrote in the *New York Times Magazine* that evangelical Christians believe Bush is a "messenger from God." In truth, they regard him merely as "one of us." Bush doesn't think he speaks for God or was divinely chosen to be president. But he does believe that God works in his life and everyone else's. "That's very different from saying that the president is chosen to be president of the United States," Gerson said. Some evangelical Christian leaders insisted after the 2004 election that Bush won on the votes of Christians and was obligated to pursue their agenda of social conservatism as his top priority. But Warren told Bush the opposite when he visited the White House after the election. "You don't owe us anything," he said. "We voted for you because of who you are and what you believe."

Bush has been more powerfully affected by his faith than any other president, with the possible exception of Jimmy Carter, a born-again Christian. And his faith has had an enormous impact on his policies, certainly more than Carter's faith had on his policies. In Bush's case, there's a direct link between his personal religious experience and his support for a faith-based initiative, the program of providing government support for religious groups that work with drug addicts, alcoholics, the homeless, the unemployed, prisoners, and the dysfunctional.

Bush knew how faith had changed his life and saw faith-based organizations, most of them Christian, achieving extraordinary results that exceeded those of government social service agencies. As governor, he locked arms and sang hymns with prison inmates and kept Teen Challenge, which treats addicts through conversion to Christianity, from being shut down by bureaucrats. While campaigning in Iowa in 2000, Bush showed up at a Teen Challenge treatment center. "I'm just like you," he told the recovering addicts. "I'm on a walk. It's a never-ending walk. I used to drink too much, but I quit. Billy Graham planted a seed in my heart—he was the messenger. So I want you to know your life's walk is shared by a lot of other people, even someone who wears suits."

In his campaign autobiography, *A Charge to Keep*, Bush described the faith-based approach as "the next bold step in welfare reform." And a month after declaring his candidacy in 1999, he proposed a vast initiative to encourage contributions to religious groups that work with the poor and troubled, to unleash "the armies of compassion," and to make it easier for faith-based groups to operate and obtain government grants. The initiative became a top priority for Bush and justified his claim to be a "compassionate conservative." Here again, Bush showed that he was the "different kind of Republican" he billed himself to be in the 2000 campaign. The faith-based initiative was a revolutionary approach to social services, tapping successful private programs and downgrading government efforts larded with bureaucracy. With this proposal, Bush was turning his back on the liberal initiatives that had ruled in Washington since the days of the New Deal, which held that the government—along with taxpayer money—was the solution to every problem. At the same time, though, Bush was also pushing conservatism in a new direction, suggesting that the private sector alone could not address every need, and that government could be used as a tool to effect change.

But unlike Bush's tax cuts and education reform program, the faith-based initiative drew quiet but strong opposition in Congress—from bureaucrats, liberals, secularists, the gay lobby. The main objection was that it would fund religious Christian programs that, in turn, could discriminate in hiring against nonbelievers and gays. When it failed to pass, Bush settled for implementing a portion of the initiative by executive order. At that point, the full faith-based program slipped from the top of Bush's agenda. In 2005, when a White House official listed the most significant issues of Bush's presidency, faith-based wasn't on the list. It was mentioned only as part of the president's affirmation of "the role of religion in our common life." Bush was criticized by David Kuo, a former faith-based official, for giving up too easily. Whether the charge was true or not, the president decided to invest his political capital in other issues. But he told me that faith-based remains "one of our top domestic initiatives. My hope is it will be a lasting legacy."

The influence of Bush's commitment to Christ as his Savior has extended well beyond social services. At a meeting with his speechwriters before his State of the Union address in 2003, the president struggled with how to express his espousal of the idea that freedom was a universal, global value. Suddenly he blurted out that liberty wasn't an American contribution but was "God's gift" to the world. That clicked with Bush and the speechwriters. (The president proudly takes credit for the insight. "This was not a Gerson," he told me, referring to his speechwriter. "This was a George W.") He concluded the address with these lines: "Americans are a free people who know that freedom is the right of every person and the future of every nation. The liberty we prize is not America's gift to the world but God's gift to humanity." Bush's faith taught him a deeper lesson. "The president believes that people are made in the image of God and therefore ought to be treated with respect and dignity and not forced to live under tyranny," Gerson told me. That's a fine sentiment, shared by many political leaders. The difference with Bush is it's not lip service. He has made it the springboard for his ambitious policy of promoting democracy around the world.

Bush has adopted a socially conscious evangelism without the liberalism that's usually attached to it. Gerson has encouraged this. The president's $15 billion program to fight AIDS globally, and especially in Africa, grew out of his faith coupled with Gerson's influence. When Bush visited Africa in 2003, his first speech was on Gorée Island in Senegal, the departure point for shipments of slaves to America. He said, "The spirit of Africans in America did not break [while] Christians became blind to the clearest commands of their faith and added hypocrisy to injustice." But "all the generations of oppression under the laws of man could not crush the hope of freedom and defeat the purposes of God." Bush is a great admirer of William Wilberforce, the eighteenth-century British politician whose passionate Christianity led him to campaign, successfully, to end the slave trade in Britain. When the president spoke at Whitehall in London in 2003, he paid tribute to Wilberforce.

Bush's faith has also heightened his concern for the sanctity of life. Without it, he surely would have expanded federal funding of embryonic stem cell research. Bush opposes what the use of embryonic stem cells would inevitably lead to: the "therapeutic" cloning of embryos to exploit their stem cells. That would involve creating life only to kill it, he said.

THEOCRAT OR PLURALIST?

The president has been surprised by the unrelenting criticism of his faith. "He doesn't view himself as the leader of American evangelicalism and he doesn't view himself as a systematic thinker on issues of church and state," Gerson told me. Bush puts part of the blame for the criticism on himself and has asked a few prominent Christians to help him find appropriate language to express his faith without offending anyone. That may be a mission impossible. His critics—the partisan ones, anyway—are bent on attacking Bush for whatever he says and does. They make four specific points about Bush and his faith: One, he talks about religion more than other presidents have. Two, his faith has made him inflexible and filled with certainty. Three, he has invoked God to justify his policies. And four, he wants to establish a theocracy in America.

Bush hasn't responded directly to these charges. But that's the way presidents normally operate. They don't defend themselves and they don't admit error unless under duress. The theory is simple: presidents never make mistakes. Their aides do. Their cabinet members do. But presidents? Never. In reality, of course, presidents do make mistakes. But admitting them would undermine the mystique of the presidency and erode the president's effectiveness as the nation's leader. To protect the mystique, presidents should never concede that they've erred. They must never second-guess themselves in public. And Bush hasn't.

Still, the president has his own private theory about why he has been attacked over his faith. "It's a way to take a true part of my life and build a caricature that may or may not be true," Bush told me. "In other words, I think if you were a European elitist, a good way to demean an American president in the eyes of some in Europe is to say, 'Well, he's a narrow-minded Christian who believes that his way is the only way.' In other words, you take a person's religion and use it to suit your purposes." He said he constantly assures people "that this country must always maintain its great tradition of honoring all religions or no religion. . . . But I also say that I personally derive peace of mind from a relationship with the Almighty."

But what about the charges? Has Bush indulged in more God-talk than his predecessors? Not really. Clinton mentioned Jesus Christ more than Bush has, as author Paul Kengor revealed in his definitive book on Bush's faith, *God and George W. Bush*. Through 2003, Bush averaged 4.7 mentions per year of Jesus, or Jesus Christ, or Christ, compared with an average of 5.1 annually for Clinton during his presidency. Carl Cannon of *National Journal*, who has made Bush's religious life his journalistic specialty, said the president "has been by any standard more inclusive and less overtly religious than his predecessors."

In early 2003, several reporters concluded that Bush had stepped up his emphasis on his faith. Laurie Goodstein of the *New York Times* cited a "growing debate over whether the president's use of faith has gone too far." Dana Milbank of the *Washington Post* wrote that Bush "had adopted a strongly devotional tone . . . and far more openly embraced Christian theology." Actually, nothing had changed, as Kengor pointed out in his book. "Bush's references to God in this period were no more frequent than usual," Kengor wrote. It was simply the time of year when the National Religious Broadcasters Conference and the National Prayer Breakfast were held. Bush spoke to both, as he does annually. Kengor did a count. Bush made fewer references to God in that period in 2003 than he had in 2001.

The notion of Bush's iron certainty also became popular in the mainstream media. It was fueled by Ron Suskind's article in the *New York Times Magazine*, which argued that Bush had "created the faith-based presidency," in which he made decisions on the basis of his faith and instincts, not on "nuanced, fact-based analysis." And once he'd made a decision, Bush was suffused with certainty, Suskind wrote. This was similar to the complaint of Bush adversaries who urged the president to change his Iraq policy based on what they saw as facts. Bush, of course, refused.

The accusation of rigid certainty is contradicted by the president's frequent policy turnarounds. He proposed school vouchers, then gave up on them at the first sign of resistance. He changed his mind famously in 2002 when he switched from opposing a new Department of Homeland Security to proposing one. He flipped on the planned path to democracy in Iraq, deciding that only an elected Iraqi government should write the country's constitution. He changed his Medicare drug benefit plan, too, making it voluntary rather than mandatory. He disliked campaign finance reform legislation, then signed it into law. Bush's degree of certainty hardly matched Senator Teddy Kennedy's. Though Democrats lost the 2004 election, "we speak for the majority of Americans," Kennedy explained.

Foes of Bush have claimed he said that God told him to invade Iraq and that God is on America's side. No prominent politician in the United States accused Bush of this, but the president was subjected to a whisper campaign based on a statement by Mahmoud Abbas, the Palestinian leader. In 2003, Abbas said in an interview with an Israeli journalist that Bush had told him that God had ordered the American president to topple Saddam. White House aides suggested that a bad translation had left Abbas, whose English is poor, with the wrong impression of what Bush had said. In truth, the president has studiously avoided any claim of God's intervention. The closest he came was a line at the end of his speech to the nation on September 20, 2001, nine days after 9/11. "Freedom and fear, justice and cruelty, have always been at war, and we know that God is not neutral between them," the president said. Still, critics have insisted that his policies clash with Christ's teachings and they have questioned how Bush could know God's will. "In doing so, of course, they too were presuming to know God's will," Kengor wrote, "and that God was on their side."

The most sweeping charge—and the most absurd—is that Bush wants to set up a theocracy in America. Liberal columnists threw the T-word around recklessly. But what kind of theocracy would it be? Bush is ecumenical and pluralistic.

To the dismay of some Christians, he said Muslims pray to the same God as Christians. He went to Catholic and Protestant prayer breakfasts. Just after the 2004 election, he celebrated Ramadan at a dinner at the Islamic Center in Washington. When he talked about churches, he routinely mentioned synagogues and mosques as well. He was the first president to utter the word *mosque* in an inaugural address. And when he talked about people of faith, he also spoke kindly of people of "no faith at all." Before his speech on September 20, 2001, he spent hours meeting and praying with two dozen religious leaders—Catholic priests, Protestant pastors, Islamic clerics, a Sikh, two rabbis.

In speeches, Gerson once commented, the president has "tried to apply a principled pluralism. We have set out to welcome all religions, not favoring any religions in a sectarian way." Addressing the theocracy charge head-on, Gerson stated, "Banning partial birth abortion and keeping the status quo of hundreds of years on marriage are not the imposition of religious rule." Or even close to it.

THE BULLY PULPIT

Unlike previous presidents, Bush applies rigid rules to references to religion in speeches. Gerson revealed the rules for the first time when he spoke, shortly after Bush's reelection, to a conference organized by Michael Cromartie of the Ethics and Public Policy Center. He said the mention of religion was permissible in five specific instances and no others.

The first occurs at times of disaster, natural or man-made, when the president must give comfort to those in grief or mourning. When suffering is unfair—9/11, the space shuttle disaster, and Hurricane Katrina come to mind—"a president generally can't say that death is final and separation is endless and the universe is an echoing, empty void," Gerson said. A president must offer hope. And Bush did when he spoke at a 9/11 service at the National Cathedral on September 14, 2001. "This world [God] created is of moral design," the president said. "Grief and tragedy and hatred are only for a time. Goodness, remembrance, and love have no end, and the Lord of life holds all who die and who mourn." This speech, perhaps because it dealt with 9/11, drew no criticism.

President Bush also invoked God in his September 2005 speech in the wake of the devastating Hurricane Katrina. Addressing the nation from New Orleans, he declared, "Across the Gulf Coast, among people who have lost much and suffered much and given to the limit of their power, we are seeing that same spirit: a core of strength that survives all hurt, a faith in God no storm can take away, and a powerful American determination to clear the ruins and build better than before." The president added, "These trials have also reminded us that we are often stronger than we know with the help of grace and one another. They remind us of a hope beyond all pain and death—a God who welcomes the lost to a house not made with hands."

Another time when religious language is acceptable is when a president discusses "the historic influence of faith on our country," said Gerson. Faith provided the moral underpinning for the antislavery cause, the civil rights movement, and the pro-life movement. "We argue that it has contributed to the justice of America [and] that people of faith have been a voice of conscience," Gerson added. The Gorée Island speech falls into this category.

Bush's faith-based initiative is an obvious subject that legitimizes references to religious faith. And he has seized the opportunity. "This is rooted in the president's belief that government, in some cases, should encourage the provision of social services without providing those services," Gerson said. "And some of the most effective providers, especially in fighting addiction and providing mentoring, are faith-based community groups." Just days after his inauguration in 2001, Bush alluded to his faith-based program with these words: "Men and women can be good without faith, but faith is a force for goodness. Men and women can be compassionate without faith, but faith inspires compassion. Human beings can love without faith, but faith is a great teacher of love."

Thanks to Gerson and fellow speechwriters John McConnell and Matt Scully, Bush has often made what Gerson called "literary allusions to hymns and Scripture." Sometimes the president didn't need his speechwriters to do that. And sometimes the press didn't understand the allusion. In an interview during the 2000 campaign, Bush said people should take the log out of their eye before paying attention to the speck in their neighbor's eye. The next day in a front-page story in the *New York Times*, Frank Bruni wrote that this was an "unusual variation" on the saying about the pot calling the kettle black. Apparently nobody at the *Times* recognized the allusion to the Sermon on the Mount.

And finally there have been the repeated mentions of Providence, the role of God in human history. "The important theological principle here," Gerson told the conference, is "to avoid identifying the purposes of an individual or a nation with the purposes of God." He added, "We've done our best to avoid the temptation." In his 2003 State of the Union, Bush said Americans "have faith in ourselves, but not in ourselves alone. We do not know, we do not claim to know, all the ways of Providence, yet we can trust in them, placing our confidence in the loving God behind all of life and all of history."

The president rarely strays beyond these narrow confines for religious language, at least in speeches. He occasionally wanders in interviews. But other politicians and other presidents often have as well. During the 2004 presidential campaign, John Kerry spoke at Northside Baptist Church in St. Louis and cited James 2:14 in an attack on Bush: "What good is it, my brothers, if a man claims to have faith but has not deeds?" The president not only didn't make campaign speeches in churches, he also never invoked Scripture to criticize a political opponent.

President Franklin D. Roosevelt's State of the Union address in 1942 was, in part, a hymn to religion. It was just over one month after Pearl Harbor and Germany's declaration of war against the United States. "They know that victory for us means victory for religion, and they could not tolerate that," he said. "The world is too small to provide adequate living room for both Hitler and God. . . . We are inspired by a faith that goes back through all the years to the first chapter of Genesis."

On D-Day, in 1944, FDR addressed the nation in the form of a prayer: he prayed for victory. In his first inaugural, President Dwight D. Eisenhower read a prayer. "O mighty God," it began. He prayed for everyone in his administration, even for "my friends in journalism." His windup: "May cooperation be permitted with the mutual aim of those who, under our concepts of the Constitution, hold to differing political faiths, so that all may work for the good of our beloved country and Thy Glory. Amen."

Bush hasn't matched FDR or Ike, but President Carter said something Bush would identify with. "To me, God is real," he said in 1978. "To me, the relationship with God is a very personal thing. God is ever present in my life, sustains me when I am weak, gives me guidance when I turn to Him, and provides for me, as a Christian, through the life of Christ, a perfect example to emulate in my experiences with other human beings." But Carter went on to say what Bush would not and has not. "We worship freely," Carter said, "but that does not mean that leaders of our nation and the people of our nation are not called upon to worship, because those who wrote the Declaration of Independence and the Bill of Rights and our Constitution did it under aegis of, the guidance of, with a full belief in God." Such a statement would have violated Bush's rules.

Unlike Bush, Carter was not criticized for his statements, nor were FDR or Ike. Worse for Bush, he has raised suspicions that he speaks to Christians in a code that non-Christians can't understand. "I've actually had, in the past, reporters call me up on a variety of speeches and ask me where are the code words," Gerson said in his address. "I try to explain that they're not code words. They're literary references understood by millions of Americans. They're not code words. They're our culture." Such incidents have reinforced the president's sense that the national press corps is an elitist group that does not reflect, or understand, the beliefs and opinions of a broad swath of Americans. If some people don't get the allusion, Gerson pointed out, "it doesn't mean it's a plot or a secret." It's simply Bush, talking about faith in a circumscribed way that was never controversial until his opponents decided to make it so.

Bush has suffered for his faith, but he hasn't complained. His personality has been softened by his faith. Some but not all of the rough edges have been scraped away. But he's no milquetoast. A congressional ally of the president said White House aides operate in a "state of fear" that they won't meet Bush's stringent demands. And Bush can be brusque. When he was practicing a State of the Union address, the operators of the TelePrompTer couldn't get the machine to function properly. Bush snapped at them. "I'll come back when you get it right," he said. Bush returned ten minutes later and apologized to everyone, especially the TelePrompTer operators. He said a president shouldn't act that way. Presidents don't ordinarily apologize. Bush's apology was an expression of his Christian faith.

Chapter 9

The New Conservatism

A TYPICAL CONSERVATIVE BELIEVES in three things: small government with low taxes, traditional values, including the sanctity of life, and a hawkish foreign policy. Who's a typical conservative? Tom DeLay, Dan Quayle, and Ronald Reagan fit the description, as do millions of Americans who are actively involved in politics and millions more who are not.

George W. Bush isn't one of them. Often he has sounded like anything but a conservative. He has attracted supporters by appealing to their liberal instincts. Michael Gerson signed up as chief speechwriter after hearing Bush talk passionately about his concern for the underclass. When political consultant Mark McKinnon, a lifelong Democrat, met Bush in 1997, he was struck by how "different from Gingrich" Bush was. Newt Gingrich was House Speaker at the time and the country's leading conservative. Bush was governor of Texas. He and McKinnon discussed education reform and charter schools. "It wasn't 'burn government down,'" McKinnon told me. "He saw a limited role for government on issues I cared about. I was disarmed. I liked him instantly." A few months later, McKinnon agreed to become Bush's chief media consultant. He ran the TV ad campaign for Bush in 2000 and 2004. After his reelection, Bush sent McKinnon an autographed picture from the White House. "You may think you're in the ad business," Bush wrote, "but you're really a Realtor who deals in matching the right tenant with a house like this and you've done it twice, much to the benefit of our country and the world."

Measured by the conservative yardstick, Bush can't match DeLay, Quayle, and Reagan. They score 3.0, three for three. Bush gets only a 2.0. Though he is an unabashed tax cutter, he's not a small-government conservative. He favors an activist federal government. And while Bush is an unswerving conservative on traditional values, he is not on foreign policy. He would protect America's national security and its vital interests around the world. So would a typical conservative. The difference is that Bush goes far beyond that limited role and is seeking to plant democracy in countries worldwide, whether they're friendly or hostile to the United States. His democracy campaign has been called "Wilsonian" in its ambition and scope—after President Woodrow Wilson, who promoted democracy in place of autocracy and colonialism after World War I. To a typical conservative, "Wilsonian" is a slur, not a compliment. So Bush gets a half-point on taxes, one point on values, and another half-point on foreign affairs. Not bad, but hardly typical.

What kind of conservative is Bush exactly? He calls himself a "compassionate conservative," and that label is appropriate as far as it goes, which isn't very far. It applies only to a
small part of Bush's agenda, the help-the-downtrodden part.
Bush added a sentence about training lawyers in DNA evidence to his 2005 State of the Union address just to have
something resembling a compassionate-conservative idea in
there. He's also been dubbed a "big-government conservative" (by me, in fact, during Bush's first term). That does not
mean, as some conservative critics would have it, that he's
really a liberal at heart. As seen with the president's "ownership society," Bush does not hope to keep expanding government; rather, he is trying in many cases to increase individual
responsibility and thus reduce the demand for government aid
and comfort.

That is why Republican national chairman Ken Mehlman
refers to Bush as a "demand-side conservative," borrowing a
label first suggested by Jonathan Rauch of *National Journal.*
But this description, too, has its drawbacks—namely, it does
not cover the values or foreign policy aspects of Bush's political philosophy. Calling Bush a "post-Reagan conservative"
puts him in the right time frame, but it's too vague.

Bush is blunt in rejecting William F. Buckley's dictum that
conservatives should stop the advance of history. When I
asked him whether his conservative activism was the opposite
of that philosophy, Bush said, "That's right. I think the role of
a conservative—I believe strongly in what I stand for—is: let's
lead. We've got enormous influence and we have a chance

to effect peace for generations to come. I like to say we're laying the foundations for peace. The walls may be built by somebody else, but you've got to have that good, strong foundation."

The president defended, on conservative grounds, his policy of spending billions to fight AIDS, hunger, and malaria around the world. "We're using conservative principles, results-oriented policy, measurements to determine whether or not the money that we're spending is being spent wisely, because our goal is to save lives, not to enhance bureaucracies." And leading, he told me, doesn't mean "leading alone." It means that "you lead others who are with you. And this requires skillful application of diplomacy."

But Bush's leadership after Hurricane Katrina in 2005 touched off a revolt among conservatives. His answer to the disaster was characteristic: he would use the federal government to achieve a conservative end, a rebuilt Gulf Coast with a thriving economy. Bush would also replace state and local governments as first responders to natural disasters, terrorist attacks, or outbreaks of disease by deploying the military. That would require changing federal law. In the past, Washington's job, carried out by the Federal Emergency Management Agency (FEMA), was merely to coordinate recovery efforts, not take them over.

It was the vastness of the president's plan and its staggering cost that alarmed conservatives, some of whom had never warmed up to his emphasis on Washington's solutions. To attract businesses, Bush wanted to turn coastal Louisiana and

Mississippi into a federal enterprise zone with reduced taxes and fewer regulations. And besides giving away federal land, he would provide $5,000 in Worker Recovery Accounts to every evacuee. To small-government conservatives, the Bush plan was reminiscent of FDR's New Deal or Lyndon Johnson's Great Society. To them, it was one federal intervention too many.

Bush was so fixated on the devastation and suffering in the region that he failed to sense a conservative backlash. He had internalized the criticism that his administration was slow to react to Katrina, though in Louisiana, anyway, the fault lay with the governor and mayor of New Orleans. Bush took full responsibility. Faced with incompetent state and local leaders, he felt he had no alternative. In the weeks after the hurricane, he took eight trips to the region. Only belatedly did he accede to the desire of conservatives for spending cuts to cover some of the Katrina spending.

Bush's Katrina policy disturbed many conservatives because it seemed so different from traditional conservative policy. And in truth, Bush's conservatism *is* new and different. But with the possible exception of his Katrina relief program, Bush conservatism is not outside the broad mainstream of conservative thinking. In fact, because most of his brand of conservatism has caught on and the remainder is likely to, it's the conservatism of the future.

A NEW PATH

Bush conservatism has had an unexpected political impact. For two decades, Reagan gathered conservatives of every ideological permutation under the umbrella of his conventional conservatism. Now Bush, despite periodic revolts on issues like the Harriet Miers nomination, has united them again under his unique brand of conservatism.

His appeal has even reached to professional athletes. After pitcher Curt Schilling led the Boston Red Sox to victory in the 2004 World Series, he appeared on ABC's *Good Morning America* and blurted out an enthusiastic endorsement of Bush. Then he contacted the president's reelection campaign and offered to help. Red Sox officials (all Democrats) talked Schilling out of appearing with Bush in New Hampshire. "The last thing I want to do is put Curt in an awkward position," Bush told his aides. But Schilling persisted. He joined Bush in Ohio, a critical battleground state, and introduced the president at several rallies. White House communications director Dan Bartlett called Schilling "a stand-up guy."

True believers in the conservative movement have a well-earned reputation for bickering and for grousing about conservative leaders for being insufficiently conservative. M. Stanton Evans, the conservative writer, has a rule of thumb about conservatives who gain political power: once our friends are in power, they are no longer our friends. Reagan was an exception. Now Bush is, though conservatives feel free to criticize him in a way they didn't Reagan. The enthusiasm of conservatives allowed Bush to gear his reelection campaign around expanding his vote in conservative areas. He didn't compromise his conservatism by making a beeline to the political center. He counted on the wrath of the liberal opposition to drive moderates and independents his way.

But he has alienated certain elements of the conservative movement, especially paleoconservatives led by Patrick Buchanan. They recoil at Bush's internationalism, particularly his decision to invade Iraq, and his fondness for federal spending and for immigrants. Both economic conservatives and libertarians abhor the growth of government under Bush. Nonetheless, these disgruntled conservatives are part of Bush's conservative coalition, if only reluctantly. Bush doesn't take lightly challenges to his conservative credentials. In 1994, while running for governor of Texas, the state Republican chairman, Tom Pauken, issued his own welfare reform plan and declared himself more conservative than Bush. Once elected, Bush marginalized Pauken's influence.

There are two keys to Bush's ability to create conservative fusion. The first is an overriding issue. Throughout his career, Reagan had anti-Communism. It dwarfed every other issue, including the economy. Bush has the war on terrorism. It is not as towering an issue as combating Communism, but it, too, overshadows other issues. Libertarians quibble about the minor First Amendment limitations of the antiterrorist Patriot Act. But conservatives generally agree with Bush's hard-line formulation of a war against terrorists and those who harbor terrorists.

The second key is that Bush's new conservatism has something significant for nearly everyone. For economic conservatives, there are tax cuts that have brought the rates on individual income down to Reagan-era levels—and to still lower levels for capital gains and dividends. For social and religious conservatives, there's Bush's strong opposition to abortion, cloning, and gay marriage. For foreign policy conservatives, at least the idealists among them, Bush is a dream come true with his drive for democracy around the world and his reversal of America's policy in the Middle East. For compassionate conservatives, Bush's global AIDS project and his faith-based initiative are lifted from their agenda. For libertarians, there's the fight for Social Security reform, which has united Bush and the Cato Institute, the foremost libertarian think tank. For small-government conservatives, there's not much except the hope that Bush will succeed in moving America nearer to an ownership society that, in turn, shrinks the demand for government services. For paleocons, there's even less to love about Bush conservatism, but they have nowhere else to turn. In any case, they constitute a distinct minority in the conservative movement.

The question about conservatism has always been how much change in society it will tolerate. The underlying principle is that if change is not necessary, it's necessary not to change. Bush has decided change is necessary. As Texas governor, he concluded that public schools required a radical shake-up. At an education forum, Bush parried critics and spoke bluntly. His reform package, he asserted, "is the true conservative position, and if you don't like it you can vote me out of office." He was reelected in 1998.

Rather than abandon conservatism for the sake of change, Bush has redefined it to fit the times and to come to grips with political reality. The president's policy on education is a perfect example. When Reagan came to office in 1980, he proposed eliminating four cabinet agencies. The Department of Education topped the list. But efforts to kill the Education Department failed and proved to be politically counterproductive. Those attempting to get rid of the department were accused of opposing education itself. It was an unfair charge, but it worked to frighten away critics and preserve the department in perpetuity.

Bush wisely chose not to engage that battle anew. "He never gave it a thought," Sandy Kress, his education adviser, told me. Instead, with education standards and student performance declining and public schools dodging accountability, he proposed to use the Education Department to achieve conservative results. His No Child Left Behind legislation violated two conservative principles, local control of schools and minimal federal intrusion, at the same time that it promoted two others, high standards and accountability. The measure was cosponsored by Senator Ted Kennedy, but liberals belatedly realized that it reflected the rudiments of Bush's conservatism. They began demanding, in vain, that it be watered down or repealed. George Will characterized their alternative as "Let's leave lots of kids behind."

The president characterized his education policy as a "classic example" of applying conservative philosophy to "an issue that normally has been ceded to the other party." He suggested that conservatives had foolishly downgraded public education in the past. "The message was, at times, public education isn't important," Bush told me. "We said public schools are important, they've been really important throughout our history, let's make them better, as opposed to saying let's abolish them." On this issue, he said, "I hope people say this is the guy who can think through problems and figure out ways to put in place something that causes positive results."

WHAT WOULD REAGAN DO?

Bush doesn't wear a bracelet with "WWRD" engraved on it, but he's a great admirer of what Reagan did and said. In his memoir *Taking Heat*, former press secretary Ari Fleischer said he once chastised Bush for oversimplifying the war on terror as a struggle of "good versus evil." Bush strongly disagreed. "If this isn't good versus evil, what is?" he asked. Bush reminded Fleischer of the message Reagan sent to Soviet leader Mikhail Gorbachev when he visited the Berlin Wall. "He didn't say put a gate in this wall. He didn't say take down a few bricks." Reagan said, "Mr. Gorbachev, tear down this wall." Bush thought Reagan had spoken clearly and concisely and had distinguished right from wrong. "That was Reagan's style," Fleischer said. "It's Bush's too."

In transforming conservatism, Bush's policies are, more often than not, what Reagan would have done in similar circumstances. Reagan, after all, was not a stand-pat conservative. He made conservatism more assertive, populist, and optimistic. He rejected the fiscal conservatism of balanced budgets in favor of supply-side tax cuts. He readily tossed aside the arms-control policy of previous Republican presidents and wholeheartedly championed antimissile defense in his Strategic Defense Initiative—or Star Wars, as his opponents called it. When Reagan met with Gorbachev in 1986, he boldly proposed to abandon all nuclear weapons in one swoop rather than laboriously negotiate reductions. And he, like Bush, gave up on abolishing cabinet departments once that task looked impossible.

Bush is not a Reagan clone. But comparing him with Reagan, the conservative standard bearer, is a way of assessing how conservative Bush truly is. So what would Reagan have done in the twenty-first century to trim the size of government and make it smaller? The answer is just what Bush has done: next to nothing. The only difference is that Reagan famously proclaimed that government was the problem, not the solution. But after gaining $35 billion in spending cuts in 1981, he gave up the fight. Reagan had a tacit agreement with congressional Democrats that he would go along with their domestic spending increases if they'd approve his defense spending hikes. And the federal government, in terms of spending, grew. David Stockman, Reagan's budget chief and a small-government zealot, found himself on the losing end of arguments over spending cuts. He was so disillusioned that he declared, in the subtitle of his 1986 book, that "the Reagan revolution failed." For Reagan, winning the Cold War trumped everything else.

Bush has never proclaimed himself a small-government conservative and hasn't ridiculed government bureaucrats as Reagan regularly did. He has explained his policy as favoring all the government that's required and no more. That leaves a lot to Bush's discretion. He prides himself on using his political capital rather than conserving it. He believes in investing his capital, as he's doing with the ownership society, with the expectation of reaping a gain later. But he hasn't spent that capital on terminating any federal agencies or programs. Reagan would not have liked the costly Medicare prescription drug benefit that Bush pushed through Congress. But Bush at least won an expansion of health savings accounts, which gives consumers more choice, and more competition in health care markets, beginning in 2010. Would Reagan have acquiesced on Medicare? Probably.

The truth is that conservative presidents frequently get a pass from conservatives on increased spending. Reagan knew this and Bush knows it too. And there's a simple explanation: with a conservative in the White House, discretionary federal spending tilts in favor of programs—defense, in particular— that conservatives approve of. "Government funding of effective teen abstinence programs is different from government funding agencies that hand out condoms to kids," a Bush aide told me. "Supporting adoption centers is different from supporting abortion clinics. Supporting antidrug efforts is different from supporting medical marijuana initiatives."

Bush has learned, however, that conservative leaders don't *always* get a pass on spending. Conservatives in Congress and the media finally rebelled when he proposed a $100-plus billion recovery program after Hurricane Katrina. The Republican Study Committee in the House of Representatives, led by Mike Pence of Indiana, claimed that the president could offset some of the cost of the recovery by cutting more than $102 billion. In the Senate, six Republicans suggested a freeze in spending that would save nearly $50 billion. Conservative columnists were scathing in criticizing Bush's penchant for spending. Peggy Noonan called the president's disaster relief effort a "boondogglish plan" and suggested that Republican leaders were beginning "to spend like the romantics and operators of Lyndon Johnson's Great Society." Jonah Goldberg wrote that he hoped the backlash against the lavish price tag for Katrina repairs might snuff out Bush's idea of compassionate conservatism.

Still, most of the president's conservative critics would recognize that on taxes, Bush is Reagan redux. Bush has invoked the same supply-side language as Reagan, promising that his tax cuts would spur the economy and let people keep more of their own money. Reagan first cut taxes, then went for sweeping tax reform—ditto Bush. Reagan ultimately cut the top tax rate on individual income to 28 percent. Bush hasn't yet matched that, lowering the rate to 35 percent. But he's out-Reaganed Reagan by reducing the bottom rate for individual taxpayers to 10 percent and the rate on capital gains and dividends to 15 percent. Neither Bush nor Reagan was swayed by apocalyptic talk about the deficit. Both concluded that a growing economy was more important than deficit reduction.

On two central issues, Bush is actually more conservative than Reagan. In 1981, the Reagan White House put together a Social Security reform plan to eliminate the minimum benefit for thousands of Americans and raise the retirement age. When the Senate passed a unanimous resolution condemning it, Reagan backed off. In 1983, he accepted a shortsighted Social Security solvency plan that increased the payroll tax and raised (gradually) the age of eligibility for full retirement benefits. Bush now confronts a system that will slip into the red by 2017. And his solution is far bolder than anything Reagan endorsed or even thought seriously about. Bush would brake the growth of benefits for the better-off and allow everyone, rich or poor, to use part of what would otherwise be Social Security taxes to invest in financial markets. This is a revolutionary approach of the sort that Reagan would surely endorse. It not only relies on the free market, it also gives individuals more choice over how to handle their own money. Free markets and individual choice were Reagan staples. On Social Security, Bush is Reagan's rightful heir.

The same is true on social issues. Reagan was a pro-lifer who spoke passionately, but not often, against abortion. Bush is much the same: he favors a ban on abortion, as Reagan did. Bush has also been confronted with three issues that Reagan was not: embryonic stem cell research, cloning, and gay marriage. Bush has opposed all three. On stem cells, he has increased the federal subsidy for research but refused to broaden the subsidy to cover a never-ending supply of embryonic stem cell lines. The fact that Nancy Reagan took exception to Bush's refusal was not indicative of what Reagan himself would have done. She was always less conservative than her husband, emphatically so on social and values issues. On cloning, there's little doubt Reagan would have firmly opposed it, even the euphemistically named "therapeutic" cloning. As for gay marriage, that's more doubtful. Bush is squeamish on the subject. He doesn't like to discuss the issue at all, much as his father hated talking about abortion. Bush was reluctant to call for a constitutional amendment to preserve traditional marriage. But he did. Reagan might not have. The bottom line: on social issues, Bush's conservatism trumps Reagan's.

On national security, Bush is indisputably Reagan's successor. Like Reagan, he's a moralist and an idealist. Reagan vigorously took on the greatest threat to America's security in his time, Communism. Bush has unhesitatingly taken on the greatest threat in his, Islamic terrorism. Reagan aided insurgencies in countries that had fallen into the Soviet orbit—Nicaragua, Afghanistan, Angola—but was selective in pushing for democracy. He subjected nondemocratic allies in the Cold War to minimal pressure, though he believed that only democracies were legitimate states. Bush has made the pursuit of democracy universal. Reagan left office before the collapse of Communism and the end of the Cold War. But the logical next step—for a conservative president, anyway—would have been a global push for democracy. That would advance America's national security interests and aid the war on terror. No doubt Reagan would have taken that step, just as Bush has.

CHOICE, ACCOUNTABILITY, AND FREEDOM

Passing the Reagan test with flying colors doesn't guarantee that Bush's redefinition of conservatism will endure. Absent a tough-minded conservative in the White House, the federal bureaucracy can marginalize policies it dislikes and discourage supporters of those policies. State Department officials tried to do just that with Bush's policy on Iraq and the use of force. "They were oftentimes not engaged in support of the policy," a senior White House official who confers with Bush daily told me. "Ambassadors who were instructed to get out there in their capitals and actively support the policy, publicly and so forth, talk about it with the press and so forth, refused on the grounds they didn't agree with the policy. They refused direct instructions to go out and support and sell the policy. . . . You didn't have the [State] department teed up and actively and aggressively supporting the policy. We didn't have effective, articulate spokesmen out there saying this is the right thing to do, this is what we're doing, and this is why we're doing it." And this near-mutiny occurred under a strong conservative president.

Yet there's reason to believe the Bush approach to foreign policy and key domestic issues, and his use of government, will stick as key elements of the conservatism of the future. The president has responded to public opinion. Bush conservatism makes political sense—and it works.

Bush vowed during his 2000 campaign that America would adopt a humbler foreign policy. And he tried it for nine months. It didn't work. The elites of the world—Europeans, Middle East dictators, leftist leaders—complain when the United States exerts its influence. The masses don't. They have gained enormously from Bush's post-9/11 policy of waging war on terrorism and demanding democratic change. The list of countries that are moving toward democracy (sometimes only inching) or have already arrived is growing: Afghanistan, Iraq, Ukraine, Lebanon, the Palestinian Authority, Egypt, Pakistan, Saudi

Arabia, Kuwait. Bush has won the argument over whether democracy is appropriate for Arab and Muslim countries. And even many doubters are coming to agree with his insistence that democracy is the best assurance of America's security. Both realist and liberal critics claim that there's no guarantee newly created democratic countries will elect pro-American or neutral governments. Bush's response: they usually do.

A conservative successor in the White House might relax the intensity of Bush's global crusade for democracy and moderate America's role as the world's policeman. But change the policy altogether? The only alternatives are a return to Bush's initial policy of humility, which failed, or to President Clinton's reliance on multilateralism, which also failed. With the terrorist threat lurking for generations, the Bush policy is the only viable option.

On domestic issues, Bush's policies are likely to endure even where they depart from traditional conservatism. That is because Bush conservatism reflects, and responds to, the political realities of contemporary America.

Consider, for example, the controversial issue of immigration. Bush does not agree with the many conservatives who favor a massive buildup of guards along America's southern border or those who advocate denying government services to illegal immigrants and their families. While campaigning for president in South Carolina in 2000, Bush was angered by several voters at a town hall meeting who called for draconian measures against immigration. "Family values don't stop at the Rio Grande River," he said, surprising the crowd. "If you're a mother and father with hungry children, you're going to try to put food on the table. That's reality. That's called love." Bush has been steadfastly pro-immigrant for years. In 1994, he went out of his way to express opposition to the ballot referendum in California called Proposition 187, which sharply curtailed access to public services for illegal aliens. (California voters approved it handily.) At a White House meeting on immigration in 2005, "the president spoke more passionately than I've ever heard him on any issue," an aide told me. Bush's remedy would allow thousands of immigrants to work in the United States in hopes that this would curtail border crossings by illegal aliens.

Despite being at odds with many fellow conservatives' views, Bush's immigration policy is likely to stick. The politics of immigration, more than Bush's sentimental view of immigrants, make it so. Hispanics are the fastest-growing voting bloc in the country, and in recent elections the Hispanic vote has been drifting to the Republican Party. Bush's percentage of the Hispanic vote in 2004 was 44 percent, up from 35 percent in 2000. Many Hispanics identify with the cultural conservatism, entrepreneurial spirit, and patriotism of Republicans. But they also want to feel welcome in America, and Proposition 187 drove a wedge between Hispanics and the Republican Party. Bush and his brother Jeb, the governor of Florida, have fought to make the party inclusive and remove the wedge.

In his 2002 reelection campaign, Jeb Bush broadcast a powerful TV ad that flashed Latin American flags, after which Bush came on the screen and said how happy he was so many Hispanics had come to America and become citizens. When the ad was shown to Hispanic focus groups, the participants asked to see it again and again. Jeb Bush won the Hispanic vote overwhelmingly. At the national level, the Republican majority coalition is dependent on preserving a solid share of the Hispanic vote. This alone means that a pro-immigrant policy is likely to be a lasting Bush legacy.

Politics is also at the center of Bush's education policy. For decades, education was regarded as a Democratic issue. Bush changed that. By concentrating on education reform as Texas governor and president, Bush neutralized the Democratic advantage. He remade Republicans as the party of reform by using the Education Department the same way a conservative president routinely uses the Treasury Department or the Defense Department—to achieve conservative ends. He's made the right enemies: the two teachers' unions and other enemies of accountability. It makes no sense for conservatives to roll back that policy now to accommodate a small-government theology that may work in theory but, on education, hasn't in practice.

One of the virtues of conservatives is their ability to take the world as it really is. Nonetheless, many conservatives cling to the hope that someday, somehow, the federal government will be substantially reduced in size. This is a fantasy, or at least a goal for the far-off future. The possibility of smaller government has been tested twice in the past quarter-century, first with the Reagan Revolution following the 1980 election, then with the Gingrich Revolution after 1994. Both revolutions led to a single year of meaningful spending cuts, then a return to sizable annual increases, with departments and agencies targeted for extinction still intact. Reagan and Gingrich failed for lack of public support. As George Will has pointed out, a conservatism that advocates a strong role for government—Bush-style conservatism—is now "the only conservatism palatable to a public that expects government to assuage three of life's largest fears: illness, old age, and educational deficits that prevent social mobility." As Will suggested, the traditional measurement used to separate Democrats from Republicans—"big" versus "small" government—simply doesn't work well any longer.

Bush and his aides have embraced an insight lost on some other conservatives: what matters is not how big government is but what it does. Liberal policies caused dependency, a Bush official told me, "and in the process corroded the character of the citizenry." But Bush realized that a conservative president can use government policies to expand personal freedom, a conservative virtue. His reforms to create voluntary investment accounts in Social Security and health savings accounts in Medicare aim to do that.

A fair question, though, is whether Bush conservatism is philosophically coherent. Proposing to reduce Social Security's unfunded liability, as Bush has, just after ballooning Medicare's with a prescription drug benefit is hardly coherent. Nor does it make sense to sign a lavish farm subsidy bill, which Bush did, while advocating fiscal restraint. The coherence rests with the three words and one institution that sum up Bush conservatism. The words are *choice*, *accountability*, and *freedom*. The institution is a strong national government.

These themes hang together and constitute a sensible new conservatism.

The choice thread runs through Bush's domestic policies. Their aim is to create more individual choices in the major decisions of one's life. Through tax cuts and tax reform, an individual would have more control over his own income and how to spend it. With Social Security reform, an individual would choose how to invest part of his payroll taxes. With health care reform, an individual would choose his insurance and where and how much to spend on medical care. Education reform allows individual parents, in limited cases, to choose an alternative to a failed school. Lifetime savings accounts would give individuals more choice in how much to save and when and how much to spend. The expansion of choice is consistent with modern trends. The 401(k) and IRA revolution has changed the way individuals save, invest, and finance their retirement. They choose, employers don't. The Bush revolution in domestic policy means individuals would choose, not government.

Institutions shun accountability, none more than America's public school system. School boards and administrators and teachers don't want to be graded on the basis of the performance of students. It's easy to see why: student performance has nosedived. Also, unions as a rule oppose anything that has union members competing against one another. Bush's education package, with required testing of elementary school students, would hold education officials accountable. The reasonable assumption is that accountability will lead to improved teaching and learning. Bush has also expanded competitive bidding for federal government work now done by more than 450,000 bureaucrats. This is a way of holding them accountable. If they can't measure up, their jobs will go to the private sector. And the president has injected accountability into his foreign policy. Nations are held accountable for moving to democracy—often in public, by the president or Secretary of State Condoleezza Rice. Bush said in early 2005, "We will consistently clarify the choice before every ruler and every nation, the moral choice between oppression, which is always wrong, and freedom, which is eternally right." With Bush, results matter. And accountability is a means of producing good ones. He and Rice have made it clear to leaders like Hosni Mubarak of Egypt and Vladimir Putin of Russia that the closeness of their relationship with the United States will depend on their support for democracy.

For presidents, freedom is normally a watchword and an ideal. For Bush, it's a policy and a doctrine: the more freedom for individuals at home and abroad, the better for America and the world. It's especially applicable to the Middle East. Attempts to impose stability there without freedom have failed. "The core of [Bush's] doctrine rests on the president's belief that stability cannot be purchased at the expense of liberty," explained Peter Wehner, the director of the White House Office of Strategic Initiatives, in a speech to the Hudson Institute in Washington. "As long as the Middle East remains a place where freedom does not flourish, it will remain a place of stagnation and resentment, a cauldron of anti-Western hatred and violence."

Bush has fashioned a theory of democratic elections. Even

if, as his critics claim, elections aren't the same as democracy, he believes the process of holding elections produces the building blocks of democracy—political parties, civic habits and institutions, an engaged electorate, an active press, and the delegitimization of the enemies of democracy.

When I asked the president about his views on this subject, he said that elections are only "the beginnings of democracy" but that the importance of those beginnings should not be overlooked. Even in the short term, he argued, elections have a powerful effect, since they offer "a way for people to defy killers without using weapons." Moreover, he said, elections build "civic structure" and also "affect the psychology of a country" because they "raise hopes." Bush stressed that "democracy takes a while," which is something that critics fail to realize because "we're living in impatient times," he said. "Of all people who should be patient about the development of democracy, it's America," he told me. "It took us a long time, and we're still working on it. That's the great thing about democracy."

"Not since Lincoln has the putative head of the Republican Party so actively sought to ground the party in a politics of natural right," wrote political scientists James Ceasar and Daniel DiSalvo in the influential quarterly *The Public Interest*. That natural right is freedom.

Trying to categorize Bush conservatism is difficult but not impossible. Over three decades, Bush has been ahead of other political leaders in attaching himself to some extraordinary ideas. Bush broached Social Security reform for the first time when he was running for the House of Representatives in

1978 (and losing). Education reform was a product of his campaign for governor of Texas in 1994. The emphasis on individual choice grew out of his presidential campaign and first White House term. No doubt partly from watching his father flounder in the presidency, Bush seized hold of the idea of a strong national government led by a commanding president.

In his 1999 campaign autobiography, *A Charge to Keep*, he described the role he expected to play as president. "My job is to set the agenda and tone and framework, to lay out the principles by which we operate and make decisions, and then delegate much of the process to [my staff]," he wrote. Put succinctly, it meant that Bush would be in charge of everything except details. He has been. He has thwarted terrorism, changed parts of the world forever, dominated Congress, curtailed federalism, won fundamental reforms, and treated critics as a nuisance—all of it made possible by a strong national government. "It's possible to believe in a limited government that is also strong," the Republican National Committee's Ken Mehlman told me. Bush believes that, and in this regard he is more the heir to Alexander Hamilton than to Thomas Jefferson, the usual conservative favorite.

Bush, then, is best characterized as a strong-government conservative, a label coined by journalist and speechwriter Dan Casse. Given Bush's influence, many more conservatives will adopt that label and the ideology that goes with it. After all, it was on Bush's watch and because of his assertive leadership and special brand of conservatism that Republicans became America's majority party for the first time since the 1920s.

Chapter 10

The New Majority

PRESIDENT BUSH ONCE DISCLOSED a succinct political strategy. "You can fool some of the people all of the time," he said, "and I'm going to concentrate on those people." It was a joke, reflecting Bush's easygoing West Texas manner and habit of not taking himself too seriously.

John Kerry, rich and Eastern, lacked the laid-back style popular in the Southwest. Still, it seemed he and the Democrats would have enough advantages to overcome that deficiency in 2004. New Mexico in particular offered real opportunity. The state had leaned Democratic since the 1930s. Democrats led Republicans in registration by 50 percent to 33 percent, and that included Republican gains since 2002. In 2004, Democrats controlled the governorship and both houses of the state legislature (Senate 24–18, House 42–28). Kerry seemed to have an additional edge because New Mexico is a majority-minority state (42 percent Hispanic, 9 percent American Indian, 2 percent black, 1 percent Asian-American). Democrats had won the last three presidential races in New Mexico. Though Al Gore had won the state by a mere 366 votes out of nearly 600,000 cast in 2000, Kerry fielded a far stronger campaign in New Mexico than Gore had.

Indeed, Kerry's New Mexico campaign was a masterpiece. To begin, he visited that key battleground state frequently. More important, Democrats conducted an extremely successful voter registration drive on his behalf. Bill Richardson, the popular and politically sophisticated governor, put together an organization, Moving America Forward, to supplement the massive registration effort of America Coming Together, the national independent expenditure outfit funded by billionaire financier George Soros and other wealthy Democrats. Both groups used paid workers. Richardson practically guaranteed a Kerry victory. On top of that, Democrats got a break when the secretary of state, a Democrat, told registrars that they didn't have to enforce a state law requiring a picture ID at registration. Republicans took the matter to court, but the New Mexico Supreme Court ruled against them. How many ineligible voters, if any, wound up casting ballots? No one knows, but Republicans believe the number could be as high as 15,000.

The combined Democratic campaign—Kerry, the Democratic Party, Richardson, America Coming Together—produced astonishing results. In Bernalillo County, which consists mostly of Albuquerque, Kerry improved on Gore's margin over Bush in 2000 by 6,586 votes. In Santa Fe County, site of the state capital, he increased the margin by 10,565 votes. And in Taos County, Kerry beat Bush by 3,026 more votes than Gore had. Michael Barone, the political demographer and analyst, said Santa Fe and Taos were overrun with rich liberals of "the trust funder left" variety. Even so, the strength of the Kerry vote was surprising. Jay McCleskey, the chief Bush campaign operative in New Mexico, said if he'd been told that Kerry would so dramatically increase the Democratic turnout in Albuquerque, much less in Santa Fe and Taos, he'd have assumed that Bush had no chance to defeat Kerry in the state.

Yet Bush won. He topped Kerry in New Mexico by 5,966 votes. It was one of only two states that Bush lost in 2000 and won in 2004 (the other was Iowa).

How did it happen?

The Bush campaign, relying on highly motivated volunteers, got more new or occasional voters to the polls than the Democratic forces did. Each week, the national Bush campaign established voter-contact goals for New Mexico: phone calls, home visits, completed new registrations. Each week, the initial reaction of the state campaign was that the goals were unreachable. But each week the Bush volunteers met the goals or came close. They more than compensated for Democratic gains by turning out thousands of new voters in the exurbs on the fringe of Albuquerque, in rural areas and small towns, and in the region of eastern New Mexico known as Little Texas, once dominated by conservative Democrats. And Bush made deep inroads into the Hispanic vote, which Democrats thought belonged to them by long voting tradition. According to exit polls, the Bush share of the Hispanic vote rose to 44 percent in 2004 from 35 percent in 2000.

The Bush campaign sought out Hispanic voters in the same places where their volunteers made contact with Anglo voters. The reelection team focused particularly on the exurbs, where thousands of younger, transient, middle-class Hispanic families had settled. The Bush strategy was to ignore the older Hispanic communities in northern New Mexico— Taos, Santa Fe—where voters had long been part of the Democratic base. In the fast-growing communities outside Albuquerque, however, the Hispanic vote was up for grabs. And Bush grabbed a lot of it.

For the final weekend before election day, hundreds of Bush volunteers poured into the state from the president's home turf of West Texas. The volunteers included then–Commerce Secretary Dan Evans, Bush's pal from Midland. Evans was planning to leave the Bush administration in the second term, but he told Bush campaign aides that he wanted "to go working as hard for Bush as he could." Evans went door-to-door to talk to voters just like the other volunteers. "I mean here's a guy used to chauffeur-driven perks and he was just as down to earth as anyone there," state senator Rod Adair of Roswell told me. "It was a metaphor for the whole New Mexico effort, an out-of-stater joining in with an army of volunteers in the state."

New Mexico was in a sense a microcosm of the nation in 2004: the same formula—rural, exurban, and Hispanic voters— that worked in New Mexico propelled Bush to victory nationally. The president won 51 percent of the vote nationwide and produced a new majority in America—a clear Republican majority for the first time since the 1920s. America is no longer a 50–50 nation politically, as it was in the decade prior to 2004. We are now a 51 percent nation. Granted, the Republican majority is narrow and fragile. But it is nationwide and it is growing. The 55 Republican seats in the U.S. Senate are the most the party has had since 1930. The 232 House seats are the most Republicans have won on election day since 1946. And for the first time in a half-century, Republicans hold a majority of state legislative seats. They have 28 of 50 governorships, including those in the four most populous states (California, Texas, New York, and Florida). "You can drive across the nation today from east to west and north to south and never leave a state led by a Republican governor," said Republican national chairman Ken Mehlman.

Bush is responsible for pulling Republicans ahead of Democrats, a feat that eluded Ronald Reagan and Bush's own father when they were president. He has made Republicans the majority party.

But Bush gives Reagan enormous credit for showing the way. Reagan "brought a great sense of idealism and realism to the job, but he had a great sense of projecting a better tomorrow with an optimistic point of view," Bush told me. "And you can't fake optimism." Bush exudes it. "We're optimistic, we've got a vision, we've got an ideology that's good." Republicans, according to Bush, send the message that "you count more than government in the sense that we want you to decide for your own life." And he said that the Republican Party will prosper so long as it "has this sense of concern for all Americans and . . . a positive ideology that's hopeful and says our policies will make your life better, and one that has a sense of compassion."

THE REPUBLICAN ASCENDANCY

While it has taken Bush to usher in the new Republican majority, the Republican trend began in the 1980s with the election of Reagan to the White House and accelerated in the 1990s in reaction to Bill Clinton and his chaotic administration. In the realigning election of 1994, Republicans captured both houses of Congress, and they've kept control except for a brief period in the Senate in 2001 and 2002 after Jim Jeffords of Vermont defected from the GOP. Republicans also won a majority of governors' seats in 1994, including the governorship of Texas that Bush wrested from Democratic incumbent Ann Richards, and gained a plurality of state legislatures. Republican dominance at the state level has endured. In 2000, Bush actually did little to strengthen the Republican Party across the country when he won the presidency while losing the popular vote by roughly 500,000 votes. But he did not weaken the party either, and more significantly, he gave Republicans control of Congress and the White House for the first time since 1954.

The Republican ascendancy Bush sparked came in the 2002 and 2004 elections. Those were Bush elections. He was the dominant figure even when his name wasn't on the ballot in 2002. In 2000, the exit poll gave Democrats a 4 percent advantage in party identification. In the 2002 midterm election, voters identifying themselves as Republicans outnumbered Democrats by 37 percent to 35 percent. And Republicans, boosted by Bush's aggressive campaigning, defied tradition and picked up House and Senate seats. In 2004, party identification in exit polls was tied at 37 percent, the first time Republicans had matched Democrats in a presidential year since modern polling began in the 1930s.

At a minimum, this tie was proof that Republicans no longer needed to attract Democratic voters to be competitive. But a tie in party preference actually meant more than that. Moderate or conservative Democrats are more likely to vote for a Republican presidential candidate than moderate or liberal Republicans are to vote for a Democratic candidate, so a tie in party identification indicates that Republicans have the upper hand. Asked in 2005 where Republicans stood in relation to Democrats, Bush's chief reelection campaign strategist, Matthew Dowd, responded using a basketball analogy: "We have a slight lead and the possession arrow is in our favor."

If Dowd was cautious, outside observers reinforced the claim that the Republican Party was ascendant. In 2005, the Pew Research Center for the People and the Press found that "the American political landscape decidedly favored the Republican Party." Pew interviewed 2,000 voters after the 2004 election, then reinterviewed 1,090 of them in 2005. The conclusion: Republicans were in a stronger position than Democrats coming out of the election and remained stronger in 2005. "The GOP had extensive appeal among a disparate group of voters in the middle of the electorate, drew extraordinary loyalty from its own varied constituencies, and made some inroads among conservative Democrats," Pew said. "These advantages outweighed continued nationwide parity in party affiliation."

Michael Barone agreed. After the 2000 election, Barone

had said that America was evenly divided politically, with neither party having a clear majority—a "49 percent nation," he called it. After the 2004 race, he said that "the numbers have changed." Now America is "a 51 percent nation, a majority—a narrow majority—Republican nation."

The new majority fashioned by Bush is broader and more diverse than the Republican constituency of the second half of the twentieth century. In 2004, Bush won the Catholic vote (52 percent to 47 percent in the exit poll) against a Catholic opponent. The gender gap, a political phenomenon since the 1980s, practically vanished. In 2000, Gore topped Bush by 11 percentage points among women voters. Four years later, women favored Kerry by only 3 points over Bush (51 percent to 48 percent). The gain came among "mostly married, white working women with kids who live in the suburbs," said Sara Taylor, the White House political director. Bush's gain among African-American voters was only marginal (9 percent in 2000, 11 percent in 2004). But according to exit polls, the president gained 6 points among Jewish voters (from 19 percent to 25 percent)—and Republicans suspect the exit polls didn't reflect how well Bush actually fared among Jews. (Their suspicion is based on anecdotal evidence of Jewish Democrats who privately confessed to having voted for Bush.) Bush won among both high school and college graduates but lost the postgraduate vote. A favorable sign for Republicans was the growth in the percentage of voters self-identifying in exit polls as conservatives, from 29 percent in 2000 to 34 percent in 2004.

Some of these gains were ho-hum. The switch to Bush among Hispanic voters, in New Mexico and nationally, was not. It was an event of historic proportions. Hispanics are the fastest-growing voting group in the country. Democratic strategists have pointed to their rise as evidence of a renewed Democratic majority, but Hispanics, in fact, are starting to abandon the Democratic Party and vote Republican. The Republican share of the Hispanic vote rose from 21 percent in 1996 to 35 percent in 2000 and to 44 percent in 2004. The other side of this equation is that the Democratic share fell from 72 percent in 1996 to 62 percent in 2000, then to 54 percent in 2004. The new conservatism—Bush conservatism—should cause this shift to continue.

Like an astronomer who discovers a new planet, the Pew Research Center has found a distinctive new voting bloc that's a significant part of the Republican base: pro-government conservatives. This group first emerged in a Pew voter study in 1999, and its existence was confirmed after the 2004 election. "The Republicans' bigger tent now includes more lower-income voters than it once did, and many of these voters favor an activist government to help working-class people," Pew said. These pro-government conservatives account for 10 percent of registered voters and are heavily concentrated in the South. They agree with other Republicans on social issues, the importance of religious faith, and a hawkish foreign policy. Unlike low-income Democrats, they're optimistic and believe in the power of individuals to improve their own lives. But they want government to play a role. As a strong-government conservative, Bush has a special appeal to them.

Despite the Republican edge overall, Pew found that the Democratic base (44 percent of the electorate) is larger than the Republican base (34 percent). This finding was misleading. Why? Because Republicans controlled the middle ground in American politics. Voters in the political center (23 percent), Pew said, "were not particularly partisan but today they lean decidedly to the GOP." One centrist group (13 percent), called "upbeats" by Pew, is well educated and politically engaged. They voted four-to-one for Bush in 2004 and might as well be called Republicans, or at least soft Republicans. "Disaffecteds" (10 percent), another centrist group, are less well-off financially than upbeats and grumpier, and they look askance at government. They too voted mostly for Bush. "In effect," Pew said, "Republicans have succeeded in attracting two types of swing voters who could not be more different. The common threads are a highly favorable opinion of President Bush personally and support for an aggressive military stance against potential enemies of the U.S."

The ability to bring together disparate voting blocs is the defining characteristic of a majority party. These majorities may appear to be unstable, but they last for decades, until an overarching national issue intervenes to divide the party. Republicans had a governing majority from 1896 to 1932 that combined big business and the working class in cities like Chicago and Philadelphia. The Depression shattered that coalition. For a half-century, the dominance of the Democratic Party was based on a split personality: conservative Southern segregationists, Northern liberals, and Western populists. It didn't begin to disintegrate until the civil rights movement erupted and the Vietnam War soured in the 1960s.

The new Republican majority makes more ideological

sense than its Democratic predecessor. For now, there's no paramount national issue that splits Republican ranks, only smaller ones, such as immigration, abortion, government spending, and the role of religious faith in politics and policy making. But there is an issue, national security, that unites them. So long as terrorism is a serious threat, it will remain the tie that binds Republicans.

Explaining his defeat in 2004, John Kerry said the 9/11 terrorist attacks had changed the nature of the race. He was right. But it wasn't only the attacks themselves that affected the campaign. Bush's response to the attacks had an extraordinary impact.

Bush declared war on terror, ordered the invasion of Afghanistan, and routed al Qaeda terrorists and the Islamic extremist government of the Taliban. That was followed in 2003 by the invasion of Iraq and the seizure of Saddam Hussein. The president also said the terrorist threat was so compelling that the United States might have to stage preemptive strikes on countries, like Iraq, that were threatening but hadn't attacked the United States. And Bush said the battle against terrorism wouldn't be won quickly but was "generational." Because of 9/11, national security emerged from the political shadows as a major issue for the first time since the Cold War ended in 1991. And Bush's response elevated the issue even further. This aided his reelection and Republicans in general. In a wartime atmosphere, voters tend to trust Republicans more than Democrats to protect the nation from external enemies. They tend to favor a "strong leader" in the White House. In 2004, that was Bush, not Kerry.

TURNING THE MAP RED

Describing the geography of the Republican majority is easy. The red Republican states are shaped like a giant "L." It blankets the Plains and Rocky Mountain states, then cuts eastward across the entire South and covers the border states of Missouri and Kentucky. The only Republican states outside the "L" are Indiana and Ohio. The blue Democratic states are situated along the Pacific Coast and in the Upper Midwest and the Northeast.

This geographic arrangement is semipermanent but not entirely static. New Mexico and Iowa leaned Democratic until 2004. Now they're swing states. Missouri and Kentucky were swing states for decades but now lean Republican. New Jersey and Illinois, once swing states, have become solidly Democratic. What's up for grabs is four states across the industrial belt—Pennsylvania, Michigan, Wisconsin, Minnesota—and New Hampshire. Bush lost all five in 2004, though Ken Mehlman believes that massive voting irregularities in Milwaukee allowed Kerry to win Wisconsin. All five states are competitive, and Minnesota has been drifting in a Republican direction. New Hampshire is a swing state that Bush might have won, as he did in 2000, if his opponent hadn't been from next door in Massachusetts.

The simplest statement of the political trend since 2000 is that the red states are getting redder and the blue states less blue. This shows up in the bluest of blue areas, cities of more than 500,000 people. Bush didn't win any of them in 2004, but he did gain 13 percent in big cities over his vote in 2000. His performance in New York City was the most impressive. His share of the vote rose from 19 percent to 24.3 percent. His best boroughs were Brooklyn (16.3 percent to 24.5 percent) and Queens (22.6 percent to 27.7). He actually won Staten Island (46.4 percent to 56.9 percent), but it has less than half a million people. In Baltimore, his vote grew from 14.6 percent to 17.2 percent. The gains were smaller in Philadelphia (18.3 percent to 19.3 percent), Memphis (25.6 percent to 26.6 percent), Chicago (17.6 percent to 18.3 percent), and Las Vegas (45.7 percent to 46.7 percent). Too much should not be made of these pickups, but they do confirm a trend.

Stronger evidence is what happened in America's one hundred fastest-growing counties, all but three of which Bush carried in 2004. His advantage over Kerry in these counties was an astounding 1.72 million votes—half his total margin of victory. Most of these counties are exurban communities outside inner cities and older suburbs. They've experienced explosive growth over the past two decades. "They represent a compounding asset whose value for the Republican Party has increased with each election," wrote Ronald Brownstein and Richard Rainey of the *Los Angeles Times*, who studied Census Bureau and electoral data. "Bush's edge in these 100 counties was almost four times greater than the advantage they provided Bob Dole," the Republican presidential nominee in 1996.

Big Democratic-leaning counties barely grew in recent years, and urban counties lost population. But the rapid growth of exurbia is "providing the GOP a foothold in blue Democrat-leaning states and solidifying the party's control over red Republican-leaning states," according to Brownstein and Rainey. In some states, the massive turnout of voters in the outer suburbs has more than offset the growing strength of Democrats in older areas. Brownstein and Rainey took note of an important political phenomenon in the exurbs: "Identification with the GOP has become a cultural and social statement that also carries along voters who might be more open to Democrats in a less conservative environment." What should worry Democrats all the more is that the young couples who have flocked to the exurbs tend to have large families.

Exurbs, by the way, fit Bush political adviser Karl Rove's description of a typical Republican community: "Show me married couples with kids living within five miles of a Wal-Mart, a Barnes & Noble, and a Linens 'n Things, or a Home Depot with an Applebee's or a Cracker Barrel on the interstate nearby and a growing church in the neighborhood, and you've got a Republican neighborhood."

As Barone has pointed out, a huge surge in voter turnout is sometimes, though not always, a harbinger of a lasting majority coalition. In 1896 and 1932 it was. In 1952 and 1992 it wasn't. In 2004, the turnout leaped from 51 percent of eligible voters to 61 percent. Bush got 23 percent more votes than he did in 2000. Kerry received 16 percent more than Gore. So the political trajectory is unquestionably toward a larger Republican majority.

After Republicans broke out of their long-standing minority status with sweeping victories in 1994, Democrats still had favorable conditions for recovery. Despite peace and prosperity, they stalled. Starting in 2000, Republicans have had unfavorable conditions—first a recession, then a controversial war—for overtaking Democrats. They gained anyway. In 2004, as Bush won 51 percent to 48 percent, Republicans captured the total vote for House seats by 50.1 percent to 48 percent. Barone summed it up in *National Journal:* "Bill Clinton had a chance to forge a majority for his party. He failed. Bush had the chance to forge a majority for his party. He succeeded."

Clinton actually got what he worked diligently for: personal popularity. Bush was willing to surrender personal popularity to get what he sought: a transformation of American politics that made Republicans the majority party. When Bush summoned his political advisers to his Texas ranch in 2003, he told them four things were important in his reelection: one, the race would be close, more like 2000 than 1984. Two, he didn't want to win in a lonely victory that failed to elect other Republicans. Three, he favored a grassroots campaign, not one focused solely on presidential campaign appearances. Four, he wanted his legacy to be a larger and more diverse Republican Party with more Hispanics, blacks, and Jews. "We'll leave behind a party that's stronger and better," he said.

Bush's "rebel-in-chief" style helped his party. His eclectic brand of conservatism, his offhand personality, and his willingness to pursue polarizing issues didn't appeal to everyone, including some conservatives. His style was a double-edged sword. He drove Democrats and liberals crazy and prompted them to utter rash denunciations of him. But the flip side was that rank-and-file Republicans and most conservatives became enthusiastic supporters. Bush's stubborn refusal to admit error when prodded by the media enraged Democrats, but Republicans were delighted to see him thwart the arrogant press establishment. And Bush's willingness to sacrifice personal popularity for the good of his party may have had a reverse spin, actually increasing his popularity.

It was these committed supporters who became volunteers in the Bush campaign's registration drive and voter-turnout effort. Democrats thought Republican officials exaggerated the size of their volunteer army and were dubious about what it might achieve. If the Republican effort was real, they expected to see Republicans chasing after voters in the same precincts, mainly in cities and suburbs, where the Democrats were active. But they saw little evidence of Republican activity. They concluded that Democratic organizing was far more intensive—and more likely to produce results—than Republicans'. They were wrong. Roughly 1.4 million Bush volunteers were recruited, stayed active through election day, and now constitute a permanent party cadre. (The Democratic National Committee said it recruited 233,000 volunteers, but that didn't include the thousands of "paid" volunteers deployed by America Coming Together and other groups allied with the party.) Political reporters missed another Bush breakthrough: they wrote admiringly of Democratic presidential candidate Howard Dean's success in collecting 600,000 e-mail addresses of supporters. But with little fanfare, the Bush campaign amassed an e-mail list of 7.5 million names.

Contrary to expectations, the Bush volunteers didn't target swing voters. There weren't enough of them. During the

1990s and the early Bush years, independents dipped from 16 percent of the electorate to 7 percent. Political reporters fell for the idea that they'd been driven to one party or another by the polarized political atmosphere. Not so. The former swing voters had, for the most part, become Republicans. Bush didn't have to worry about alienating swing voters if he appealed to his conservative base. He'd already gotten his share of swing voters. Instead, the Bush campaign concentrated on voters in the Republican exurbs and rural areas and on Hispanics. It was a strategy devised by Rove and carried out by Mehlman. Democrats didn't believe the Rove strategy could work, and some thought the whole Republican operation was make-believe. Small wonder they were surprised on election day. It worked as well nationally as it did in New Mexico.

Florida was crucial to Bush, and it has plenty of exurbs. In Clay County, outside Jacksonville, the Bush vote in 2004 soared 48 percent over 2000. Mehlman touted Pasco County, north of Tampa, as a Bush success story. The Bush vote grew 50.5 percent there. In the West Virginia panhandle, which has become an exurb of Washington, D.C., Bush won Berkeley County with a 53.6 percent increase and Jefferson County with a 49.6 percent jump. It was the same in rural counties. In Pottawattamie County in western Iowa, the Bush vote increased 30.7 percent. The Bush campaign largely ignored western Iowa in 2000, and lost that state. It won Iowa in 2004 by organizing Republican voters there as never before.

In New Mexico, it was the same story. In Rio Rancho, a burgeoning exurb of middle-class families north of Albuquerque, the polling places at Cibola High School and Paradise Hill Community Center, which normally would close at 7 P.M., stayed open past 9:30 P.M. to accommodate voters. Even more amazing was the Republican turnout in the eleven rural eastern counties, the Bush base in New Mexico. "They have stagnant growth or are losing population," state senator Rod Adair told me. "Despite that, turnout actually grew by 10 percent." In 2000, the growing counties of northern New Mexico—the Democratic base—gave Gore a 2,032-vote advantage over the eastern counties. In 2004, the eastern counties topped the northern by 1,937 votes. It was a remarkable swing.

A big rural vote was one part of the Bush strategy. But in New Mexico the indispensable part was winning over Hispanics. Kerry's out-of-state team made a rare mistake in referring to Hispanics as Latinos in ads and phone banks. That label is popular in California. In New Mexico, the preferred term is *Hispanic*. "There was no Hispanic effort," Bush campaign official Alexis Valdez told me. "It's not a monolithic vote." But the campaign did mount a Catholic effort with Hispanics in mind. It emphasized conservative social values and patriotism. That worked and may again. The volunteers are "still motivated, still ready to work, still disciplined," Jay McCleskey, the Bush campaigner in New Mexico, insisted. Patrick Rogers, the campaign's legal counsel, added, "I believe the next election has the potential for turning things around for decades to come."

That's true in New Mexico and true in the rest of America. Thanks to Bush, a Republican era is now at hand.

Epilogue

A Rebel's Legacy

WHEN I WENT TO INTERVIEW President Bush just before his August vacation in 2005, he was waiting for me. I'd gotten a call at my office to the effect that Bush was running ahead of schedule. This was uncharacteristic of a president, indeed of politicians in general. But for Bush, it is common; operating efficiently is a source of pride and a distinguishing mark of his presidency. I hurried over to the White House. The president was standing in the Oval Office, unperturbed but ready for the interview.

Once in the hour-long session and once more as I slowly moved toward the door to leave, the president raised a subject I hadn't asked about or expected to hear him discuss. It was George Washington. Bush noted that three books had recently been published about Washington, at least two of which he had read—*1776* by David McCullough and *His Excellency* by Joseph Ellis. All three books, Bush noted, "analyze his position in history. And I'm the forty-third guy, he's the first, and they're still analyzing the first." His point was that it's impossible to know what history's take will be on his own presidency. If the verdict on the first president isn't chiseled in stone, history's judgment on Bush, who has not even completed his second term, consists of nothing but conjecture. And Bush asked, about himself, the questions that historians will ask years from now: "Does his philosophy work? He had this optimistic view of the future; well, when the future gets here, was he right to be optimistic?"

We don't know the answers. But we do know a lot about the Bush presidency, a lot about his unique presidential style, his precedent-shattering approach to foreign affairs, and his no less radical domestic policy. We know some of his policies have worked in the short run. His tax cuts, for instance, helped lift the economy out of the doldrums. And his foreign policy liberated Afghans and Iraqis from the grip of tyranny. What we don't yet know is whether Bush made the world a better place, permanently. The jury is out on that. This puts Bush in a different category from Washington. We know that the world became a better place for Washington's having lived. What historians quibble over today is how much better.

Bush's presidential style is brisk, confident, and uncompromising, which irritates his opponents. Sometimes his unyielding approach upsets his supporters, too. But that's the cost of doing business, he feels. His rebel-in-chief style of governing was captured by a comment he made to me in the interview: "If you think you're right, you just stand by your guns." He flipped only once on a big issue, dropping his opposition to a Department of Homeland Security and cunningly exploiting the issue to beat Democrats in the 2002 midterm election. He also allowed Supreme Court nominee Harriet Miers to withdraw her name from consideration after vowing, in private meetings with senators, to stick with her no matter what. Bush did not bend to the will of conservative interest groups. He acceded to political reality; Republican senators told him that support for Miers was quickly eroding.

Bush is a big-picture person, eager to concentrate on major issues and delegate smaller ones. That explains why he let Laura design the Oval Office rug. He treats Washington, D.C., like a detention center and is no admirer of Congress. Bush has set records for days spent outside the nation's capital by a president. He makes no excuses for this.

Bush's emphasis on foreign policy is not unusual. Like many of his predecessors, he entered the White House with little interest in it, but soon enough and largely because of 9/11 he became a foreign policy president. But unlike some other presidents, he is not afraid to pursue policies that enrage so-called world opinion. He nixed a global warming treaty and eventually cooled the world's desire to impose coercive steps to limit greenhouse gases. He tossed out the Anti-Ballistic Missile Treaty with Russia and rejected a world criminal court. His war on terror and invasions of Afghanistan and Iraq changed the world, prompted a wave of democratic ferment in the Middle East, and spurred progress toward a settlement between Israel and the Palestinians. And he tilted America's strategic interests toward India, Japan, and Australia and away from Western Europe. This sounds like a century's worth of change.

On domestic policy, Bush is more important for what he has proposed and fought for than for what he has achieved. True, he got tax cuts and significant reforms in public education. He cracked down hard on possible terrorism in the United States, upsetting liberals and libertarians. He is a reliable social conservative, opposing abortion, cloning, and gay marriage. His two big projects, however, are incomplete. His plan to reform Social Security was stymied in 2005, but not killed. And his effort to move the ideological balance of the federal courts to the right is ongoing. He got conservative John Roberts on the Supreme Court, then seemed to take a detour by nominating Harriet Miers. But Miers's withdrawal and the appointment of Samuel Alito indicated that Bush was getting back on course. For these efforts, many conservatives embrace President Bush, despite his failure to make even a feeble attempt at cutting federal spending.

Make no mistake, though, Bush is redefining conservatism for a new era, consciously moving away from certain precepts that have traditionally characterized the conservative movement. Most notably, his championing of "results-oriented" government (a term he used several times in the course of our interview) breaks from the traditional conservative view, which he characterized succinctly: "basically, the federal government has no role." In the process, he has also brought about a new conservative majority in this country.

We can say this with confidence: Bush is a president of consequence. Many aren't. His father and Bill Clinton and Jimmy Carter were not. Nor, to be honest, was John F. Kennedy. Bush achieved big things, though some of them, like

Iraq, could be undone. And he tried to do even bigger things, like spread democracy across the globe. But how successful will Bush be over the long run? That won't be known for decades.

But is there a way to render a preliminary judgment on the Bush presidency? There is, thanks to Fred Greenstein, a professor emeritus of political science at Princeton. Greenstein is largely responsible, with his book *The Hidden-Hand Presidency*, for revising the view of Dwight Eisenhower's presidency upward. More recently, he has devised six measures for judging the success or failure of presidents in a nonpartisan, nonideological way. Of course, he has used his yardstick to measure former presidents, but I'll apply it to Bush.

Here are the six measures: public communication, organizational capacity, political skill, vision, cognitive style, and emotional intelligence. Bush is no Tony Blair in speaking off the cuff or at press conferences. But he's delivered five or six of the most important and eloquent presidential addresses of the last half-century. They will be quoted for years to come. So on public communication, Bush gets a high grade.

He also scores well on organizational capacity. It turns out having an MBA helps in running the White House crisply and efficiently. Realizing that he doesn't have to manage the entire government makes the job easier.

Political skill: getting elected and reelected indicates he has plenty. And getting most of his legislative initiatives through Congress has been impressive. But his commendable penchant for big issues also leads him to overreach at times, such as by pursuing Social Security reform absent an imminent crisis threatening the solvency of the system. And he has alienated Democrats to a degree that they aren't around when he needs them. Ultimately, though, Bush gets in more trouble when he isn't bold *enough*. For example, because he sought to avoid fights with Congress, he failed to make spending cuts a top priority and then nominated a stealth candidate for the Supreme Court, Harriet Miers. Those decisions led to bitter squabbles with conservative leaders. On this measure, then, Bush gets merely a passing grade.

Does Bush have a vision? You'd have mocked the idea in the early days of his presidency. But now he has two. One is a vision of democracy taking root everywhere on earth. His second inaugural address was the perfect expression of this vision. The other is of an ownership society.

Greenstein describes cognitive style as the way a president "processes the Niagara of advice and information that comes his way." It's not a matter of sheer brainpower. How does Bush sift and weigh and use the mountain of information he receives daily? We know enough about his leadership style to recognize that he does not get lost in the details or overwhelmed by all the information coming at him. He would never follow the model of Jimmy Carter, a relentless micromanager who, probably not coincidentally, often seemed overwhelmed by the presidency. And we know that Bush does not get bogged down by what elite opinion makers are saying, simply because he does not pay them much heed. Bush's focus on the big picture, his clearly defined principles, his desire to get things done rather than endlessly dicker in Clintonian fashion, the trust he has for his advisers—all these and other factors allow the president to assess situations clearly and make decisions easily.

Finally, there's the measure that Greenstein thinks is necessary in a president, emotional intelligence, or the ability to handle one's emotions constructively. Richard Nixon and Bill Clinton didn't have it. Bush does. Emotional intelligence may be his strongest trait. He is self-disciplined, rarely distracted, and on message nearly always.

In sum, Bush does well on at least four of the six measures. By Greenstein's yardstick, George W. Bush could well be judged a success as president. But there's one other factor that could be paramount here, that could emerge as the defining aspect of the Bush presidency.

Bush's fascination with George Washington has led him to invite David McCullough, the author of *1776*, to the White House more than once. McCullough talked seriously about the presidency at one gathering and later sat at Bush's table at the state dinner for the prime minister of India. McCullough's view of leaders is that character counts. Certainly it did in George Washington's case, as Washington's habits of character were a major factor in his emergence as a great national leader. I believe George W. Bush, though not of Washington's stature, is a man of character—decent, fair-minded, gracious, even-tempered, reliable, resolute, principled. It may make him a great leader too. And one day, probably decades from now, we'll know for certain.

Acknowledgments

THIS BOOK CAME ABOUT UNINTENTIONALLY. At the request of *Wall Street Journal* editorial features editor Tunku Varadarajan, soon after the 2004 election I wrote a piece about President Bush. It characterized Bush as an "insurgent president" who was bucking the Washington establishment and playing by his own political rules. Rafe Sagalyn, my literary agent, suggested that I could expand the one-thousand-word article into a book. I wasn't sure at first, but in drafting a proposal I saw that Rafe was right. I'm grateful to him for the suggestion.

A number of publishers were interested, but Jed Donahue of Crown Forum took the trouble to come to Washington and spend two hours talking to me about the potential book. He immediately grasped my take on Bush. I eagerly signed up to write *Rebel-in-Chief* for Crown Forum. And Jed turned out to be a skilled editor who improved the book in many ways.

It was my father, Frederic W. Barnes, who initially sparked

my interest in government and politics when I was a teenager. He was a West Pointer, an Air Force officer, a voracious consumer of news, and, after he retired from the military, an unsuccessful politician: he ran for the Virginia House of Delegates in 1963 and lost. I had planned to follow him to West Point, but once his focus shifted to politics, so did mine. I turned down an Army Reserve appointment to West Point and went to the University of Virginia instead. My father died in 1996.

My mother, Rosa M. Barnes, was just as taken with politics as my father. And she was an astute observer of the political game in Washington. Toward the end of her life, she would keep a list of political questions she wanted to ask me when we talked on the phone. She read every article I wrote for the *New Republic* and the *Weekly Standard* and critiqued them all—favorably. She died in 2005.

I might never have begun writing about politics and government were it not for Jack Germond, the great political columnist. As my boss at the *Washington Star* in 1974, he assigned me to cover Vice President Gerald Ford and then, when President Nixon resigned, to cover President Ford. I learned an indispensable lesson from Jack: that you can't really tell what's happening in politics outside Washington unless you go there. In 1979, Pat Furgurson, the Washington bureau chief for the *Baltimore Sun*, hired me as the paper's national political correspondent. It was a great job and led to my next one, writing the White House Watch column for the *New Republic*.

Michael Kinsley, then the *New Republic* editor, may wince when I credit him for influencing my political thinking. His views are as liberal as mine are conservative. But Mike was always bent on creating what he called "the new conventional wisdom." If some political figure had a lofty reputation, Mike wanted to take a skeptical look. Checking to see if the conventional wisdom has it right about a politician or a political event, I learned, is always worth doing.

The closest thing I've had to a mentor is Robert Novak. Bob is the hardest-working and best reporter in Washington. He befriended me more than thirty years ago when I was a young reporter and the only thing we had in common was a love for basketball. I haven't missed one of Bob's columns since the early 1970s, and I've learned something I didn't know from every one of them.

Then there are my longtime friends Brit Hume, Mort Kondracke, and Tom DeFrank. We've spent the past three decades or more talking about politics and policy and campaigns and political gossip. I pay attention to what they say, all the more so because they often don't agree. Two other friends, David Smick and Jeffrey Bell, taught me about the power of ideas in politics.

At the *Weekly Standard*, I'm blessed to have William Kristol as my colleague. Bill has a contrarian view of politics that, far more often than not, turns out to be right. And at Fox News, I'm fortunate to work for the man who was the smartest political consultant in the business before he left politics for news: Roger Ailes.

I'd also like to thank Erin Healy of the White House press office for facilitating my requests for interviews with nearly everyone from President Bush on down. And, of course, I thank the many individuals, in and out of the White House, who took the time to share their insights with me.

Last, I'm grateful for the loving support of my wife, Barbara, and for the unflagging interest that my daughters, Karen, Sarah, and Grace, and my son, Freddy, expressed as I wrote the book. Now they'll be forced to read it.

Index

Index

About the Author

FRED BARNES is executive editor of the *Weekly Standard* and cohost of *The Beltway Boys* on the Fox News Channel. From 1985 to 1995, he served as White House correspondent for the *New Republic*, leaving to found the *Weekly Standard* along with William Kristol and John Podhoretz. He began his career as a reporter for the Charleston (S.C.) *News and Courier*, covered the Supreme Court and White House for the *Washington Star*, and was national political correspondent for the *Baltimore Sun*. He graduated from the University of Virginia and was a Nieman Fellow for Journalism at Harvard University. Barnes lives in northern Virginia with his wife, Barbara. They have four children.